MW00586070

46 Driver

A Marine Corps Helicopter Pilot's Vietnam Memoir

by

Arnold Reiner

The contents of this book regarding the accuracy of events, people, and places depicted; permissions to use all previously published materials; opinions expressed; all are the sole responsibility of the author, who assumes all liability for the contents of this book.

Author's Note

The events in this book occurred almost a half century ago and are recounted to the best of my memory with the aid of former squadron mates and with reference to official records and documents.

International Standard Book Number 13: 978-1-60452-084-2
International Standard Book Number 10: 1-60452-084-1
Library of Congress Control Number: 2013952519

BluewaterPress LLC
52 Tuscan Way Ste 202-309
Saint Augustine Florida 32092

http://bluewaterpress.com

This book may be purchased online at -
http://www.bluewaterpress.com/46driver

Printed in the United States of America

Back cover art from: *The War in the Northern Provinces 1966-1968* by Lt Gen. Willard Pearson, Department of the Army, Washington, D.C. 1975

Introduction

These are the recollections from a sea bag of memories while serving as a Marine Corps helicopter pilot in Vietnam, as well as earlier experiences on the path to that time. The names of those in specific combat or other events affecting me directly are recounted. In more peripheral events, individuals are mentioned only by rank.

On April 22, 1966 helicopter squadron HMM-265 flew aboard the USS Boxer (LPH 4) in Norfolk, VA and a few days later, weighed anchor and steamed east to Vietnam. After brief stops in Rota, Spain and Aden, the squadron flew ashore May 22, 1966 at Marble Mountain Air Facility, a crude, single runway strip by the South China Sea adjacent to Da Nang.

At the start, there was neither optimism nor pessimism that the effort would succeed. We were simply marines executing a mission. But in retrospect, one memorable allpilots briefing at the Marble Mountain Air Facility mess hall shortly after arriving defined how optimistic and how wrong the U.S. was going to be about the war's outcome.

The briefing officer displayed a map of the northern First Corps area, commonly referred to as the "I" Corps, which was about 200 miles of coastal plain and mountains bordered by the South China Sea on the east, Laos to the west, and the 17th parallel demilitarized zone (DMZ) on the north. On the map, a red outline about 10 miles in diameter enclosed the city of Da Nang and immediate area.

The briefing officer explained that it was the tactical area of responsibility, or TAOR, and he said it would expand incrementally as marines secured the countryside. It was not to be. But sitting there in the briefing, our time in country was in multiples of hours, not even days, so we took it all in and when the briefing ended, we sauntered in the sand back to our newly erected hard back tent hooches by the South China Sea. In fact, the I Corps never became secure and as time went by, it became more contentious, particularly along the DMZ and the goal of eliminating the threat of a Communist takeover became more and more just an elusive idea. The troop assaults, medevac's, reconnaissance inserts, extractions, and logistics flights provided a bird's eye view of America's failure to achieve those goals.

As pilots we learned that untempered determination is a liability in flying and combat and that human error and mechanical failure are as dangerous as the enemy, often more so.

Acknowledgements

My thanks to squadron mates who shared their recollections and the Naval History and Heritage Command for retrieving accident records which materially aided my research and shed light on those long ago events.

Editorial Note

All photographs without attribution are from the author's private collection. Sections beginning mid-page with dropped capital letters denote the beginning of a period in the author's life.

Contents

Introduction   ix
Acknowledgements   x
Editorial Note   xi
Joining the Marine Corps Officer Program   1
Marine Corps Officer's Candidate School   5
College, the Night Shift, and Quantico   6
Flight Training   10
Checking into HMM-265 and Training   23
Helicopter Nicknames   26
The Jacksonville VFW   29
First Casualty   33
The Voyage and a Chat at the Bow   35
Coming Ashore   37
Marble Mountain and MAG 16 Heads   37
The Pilots and Off Time   40
The Mission to Dong Den Mountain   48
Relocating Villagers South of Da Nang, a Sad Scene   53
Napalm and the Farmer   55
A Quiet Day at Khe Sanh   58
Flying Backwards with Maxwell   60
Stint as a Grunt   63
Operation Hastings and Helicopter Valley   66
A Memorable Trip to Da Nang   69
R.T. and Joe Roman's Marble Mountain Crash   71

Children of I Corps   73
Looking for Pappy and Ron   76
Que Son Valley Nui Lac Son Assault   78
Unsuccessful Recon Extraction and My Purple Heart   80
Khe Sanh's Changing Scene   85
H-34 Controlled Flight into Terrain Accident   90
A Close One and Nobody Knew Nuth'n   91
Night Extraction That Thankfully Wasn't   92
A Rescue in Laos   93
Zero- Zero GCA at Phu Bai   95
Recovering the (Ryan Firebee)   99
Cubi Point Jungle Survival School   101
Aborted Medevac Mission to the Repose   104
Khe Sanh Hill 861 Medevac   107
Night Carrier Qualification   112
A Change of Plans   117
Taking KIAs Back to the Princeton   119
The Night P.T. Looney Died   120
Instrument Check   122
A Mission That Never Came to Pass   123
Coming Home   125
Appendix   129
Postscript   137
Bibliography   143
Glossary   145
About the Author   151

46 Driver

Joining the Marine Corps Officer Program

Joining the Marine Corps platoon leader officer
program at age 19 in the summer of 1960 set the
trajectory for my life. My vision at the time was to
become a commercial airline pilot and the Marine Corps
flight program, in my youthful, naïve judgment, offered the
most convenient path. Just two six-week periods of Officers'
Candidate School (OCS) in Quantico during summer breaks,
a second lieutenant's commission upon graduation, and it
was off to Pensacola for flight training. What could be easier?

Leading up to that decision was an indifferent trip
through prep school, a truck driving job in Manhattan
while taking courses at Columbia University at night, and
six months on the night shift testing high voltage power
cable at the Anaconda Copper Company's Hudson River
factory, 25 miles north of New York City. During high
school summers, I learned to fly Piper Cubs at Stormville
Airport, a small grass strip in upstate New York. As a
17-year-old flying solo over the Berkshire Hills and down
the Hudson Valley with the Cub's window open to the

summer air, I felt like I owned the countryside and those flights sowed the seeds of a flying career. I also witnessed the consequences of aeronautical hubris on a sunny June afternoon in 1958 at Stormville Airport when a stunt flying doctor crashed his Waco UPF-7 biplane into a cornfield next to the runway as I was preparing to takeoff. Seeing the crash, I cut the engine and ran toward the Waco just as its fuel tank ignited. By the time I got there, it was burning furiously with the doctor in the cockpit crumpled and charred like a marshmallow held too long over a campfire. With no crash-rescue equipment on the field, all we could do was stand there until the wreckage burned itself out. It was the first of many tragedies I'd see at the intersection of large and small human failings and the unforgiving physics of flight. The trip from those teenage Cub flights to an airline career took me back to school, into the Marine Corps, and a tenuous 13 months of war in Southeast Asia.

Deciding to go from factory worker to college student occurred on a March night during a midnight break on Anaconda's barge pier where copper ingots were offloaded and stacked before being made into power cable inside the plant. That evening, with our backs to the Hudson's dark expanse, we sat and chatted like we always did on mild evenings. The older workers were in their 20's during the Great Depression. Following Pearl Harbor, they signed up for military service or got drafted. After the war they did what their dads had done in the 1920's and 30's and got jobs at industrial plants along the Hudson. In other circumstances with family support and direction, some could have been in the professions or business. Sometimes out on the pier they told war stories, but mostly they talked about things close to home, like weekends and vacations, or a nagging job frustration. Most were married, shackled to plant work by family obligations, lack of education, and life's inertia. The man who changed my direction was about 40, a seaman on liberty ships in the war. He told of North Atlantic convoys and watching ships silhouetted against the moon that got torpedoed and sunk in the night. It seems wisdom always came in lurches to me. Listening to him on the pier that night, it occurred to me that if I kept doing what I was doing, I'd be like him, working shifts, taking breaks in the dead of night, on the pier, then ambling back through the giant freight doors into the florescent lights and hum of the factory floor. I decided to quit and return to school.

In the suburb along the Hudson just north of Manhattan where I lived, kids sometimes went to Europe after college, encouraged by parents to take time off, "see the world" and "find themselves." A prep school friend went to Germany for a year before entering college to learn the language and take in post-war European culture. When the kids returned, they seemed pretty much the same and I couldn't tell if their time abroad put them on a new path or contributed to any particular enlightenment. But my year off driving a truck and working night shifts provided the insights I needed to set course on a flying adventure I never contemplated.

Upon acceptance at the University of Bridgeport, a plain vanilla institution in a gritty Connecticut industrial town that was happy to accept students with less than Ivy League academic credentials, my next stop was the Marine Corps officer recruiting office in lower Manhattan. I had already studied the brochures and had my eye on the multi-engine training pipeline because transport planes were the closest the Marine Corps had to an airliner.

Emerging from the IRT subway on Chambers Street, a short stroll led to the old, columned building housing military recruiting offices. A gunnery sergeant in spit shined shoes, dress blues trousers, a glistening brass belt buckle, perfectly pressed khaki shirt, marksmanship badges and a chest full of ribbons ushered me in to see the officer in charge, a crisp, square jawed major with closely cropped hair and a precise, no nonsense manner. He offered me a seat. The first question was: "Why do you want to be a marine?" I explained that the Marine Corps had an aviation officer program and I wanted to get my wings and eventually become a commercial airline pilot. I would be a marine but my head and my sights were fixed beyond the Corps. He paused before responding to my honest answer. In that short silence, as the major composed his reply, he must have been thinking: "Kid you don't know what you're getting into." I obviously wasn't an ideal DNA fit for the aggressive, career marine leader the Corps was looking to recruit. The major said: "Mr. Reiner, that's not the reason people join the Marine Corps, but I think it shows sufficient motivation to get through the program. " He was there to sign up ground and flight officer candidates and had a quota to fill and I had a dream, so we satisfied each other's needs. And as things turned out, we each met our share of the bargain.

Two more preliminary steps remained before the major could notch another aviation officer candidate toward his quota and I could formalize a commitment to the Corps — a short aviation screening test and a swearing in by the major. Those completed, I left the office with a Department of Defense USMC ID card in my wallet and took the IRT subway back uptown to Riverdale. When my father, a dentist in Manhattan, got home that night, I told him that I had joined the Marine Corps Platoon Leader Class (PLC) aviation officer program and that the following summer I would be going to OCS in Quantico, Virginia. His response was just seven words: "How can you get out of it?"

Marine Corps Officer's Candidate School

Summer OCS in Quantico was heavy on physicality and tested emotional endurance and was the hardest I have ever worked. The washout rate was high, either because DI's or company officers evaluating candidates decided individuals didn't fit the bill or the candidates gave up and quit under the physical and emotional strain. A hilly forest at the Quantico base with steep furrowed paths where candidates made repeated forced marches with their packs and weapons often became the dividing line separating candidates who would become Marine Corps officers and those who would fall, sometimes literally, by the wayside. Candidates who couldn't hang in with their platoon on the increasingly more demanding hikes up and down the hill trails invariably were cut or resigned from the program.

The ability to physically confront and overpower an opponent was stressed and evaluated in one-on-one and team competitions. Not being a college team athlete like many of the PLC candidates, I didn't fare well in the pugil stick fights against stronger and more agile peers. But in team encounters where competitors carried a smaller candidate on one's shoulders and platoons fought it out in a ring, I emerged as the last one standing to the cheers of my platoon. In these "chicken fights," the hard charging football jocks hurled themselves at each other, yelling, grabbing and careening about. With Billy Rice, a comparatively light 150 or so pounder on my shoulders, we moved about on the edges of the mayhem striking opportunistic glancing blows at competitors. Within a few minutes, most candidates were down on the grass and exhausted. Finally, it was us circling in on four large jocks locked together, staggering and off balance. We rushed forward, toppling them into a heap. The lessons from these combative encounters were that head-on confrontation among equals or those of superior ability is not a strategy for success or survival. If possible, choose the time and place.

Marines have a thing about marksmanship. "Every marine is a rifleman" is right up there in the Corps' psyche with "Semper Fi," and marines proudly wear marksmanship badges to prove their shooting prowess. Marksmanship is also an item on marine fitness reports because who needs a marine who can't shoot straight? In the first Quantico OCS summer in 1961, we donned cushioned shooting jackets and spent days on the weapons range firing WWII era M1 rifles to the point our shoulders were sore from the recoil. More marksmanship training followed two years later in the second OCS summer increment. In Vietnam, I would benefit obliquely from all that time on the range.

College, the Night Shift, and Quantico

In the fall of 1961 during my sophomore year in college, my father died. I sensed my mother was feeling financially pinched, so to fund college I took a job at AVCO's Lycoming plant in Stratford, Connecticut, where they manufactured helicopter engines and ballistic missile assemblies. And because fabricating ballistic missile structures was classified work, I was investigated and, in due course, received a top secret security clearance. I found I could work either the early 3 p.m. to 11 p.m. or 11 p.m. to 7 a.m. shifts and still attend classes, get enough sleep, and study sufficiently to make satisfactory grades in my business-journalism major. As a 20-year-old sophomore more intent on flying after college, I saw the university more as an academic obstacle course than an enlightenment opportunity, akin to crossing a busy intersection without getting run over. But some of it stuck. Today, Shakespeare's characters come alive by different names in newspaper headlines and Paul Samuelson's "guns and butter" Keynesian analogies are as fresh now as when I read his textbook fifty years ago. Labor-management courses provided insights about the push and pull between companies and labor unions, a subject I witnessed firsthand earlier at Anaconda and during my time at AVCO on the night shift. And I'm grateful that I can stroll through the Metropolitan Museum of Art and better understand and appreciate what is there. On the other hand, my journalism professor, sensing my interests were elsewhere, suggested I pursue other fields. I assured him that I would.

The AVCO production area was sealed off, climate controlled, and restricted to "AUTHORIZED PERSONNEL ONLY." The job was bonding Minuteman and Titan intercontinental ballistic missile warhead heat shields to the metal under shells housing the nuclear device. Some parts were cold bonded at room temperature. But most heat shield bonding was done by three- and four-man teams pumping hot, quick setting epoxy in room-sized 150-degree Fahrenheit ovens. It was time critical work to exacting tolerances and, from start to finish, took about 15 to 20 minutes per missile warhead. Then, red faced and sweaty, we'd dash out of the oven into the relative coolness of the shop floor, our white coveralls spattered with green epoxy ooze. We drank lots of water, nevertheless, by the end of the shift we were often a dehydrated bunch lining up at the time clock to punch out. Leaving the plant, my routine was either shower and attend morning classes, or shower and sleep, depending on my class schedule.

Older workers referred to me perhaps, with a little envy, as "the college kid" and as sometimes happened, when a misstep on my part occurred, they would ask mockingly: "How could a c-o-l-l-e-g-e k-i-d...do something like that?" In the early 1960's, cold war tensions were high. The Cuban

Missile crisis was fresh in everyone's mind and nuclear armed B-52's circled in the air with target assignments, ready to penetrate Russian airspace. Missile production had ramped up in step with cold war paranoia and, thanks to that, I caught a break when it came to job assignments. Shop managers, concerned about staying on schedule and not scrapping costly heat shields due to epoxy curing mistakes, decided to assign one person on each shift to track heat shield curing cycles. Senior workers fearing repercussions if they made a mistake declined the job, and so the "college kid" got it. And what a delight it was. I devised a form matrix of oven numbers, part numbers, curing times and temperatures, to be affixed to oven doors with a parallel copy for my clipboard. No longer dealing with pumping hot epoxy resin in 150 degree ovens, my coveralls were the same white color at the end of shift as when I started. When not darting into ovens to check production tags or checking my logs on oven doors, I sat in the quality control cubicle and studied. Sometimes an oven pumping operation went bad because the heat shield got cocked on the pumping fixture, or for some other reason. In such circumstances, an all hands call went through the department to help pry the heat shield off its metal under shell before the epoxy set. It was only then that I'd leave my nest of clipboards and logs and get dirty along with the rest of the guys.

But the cushy job didn't last. With my orders to the second Quantico OCS increment in July 1963, another man more senior to me filled the slot. And discovering how easy the job was with my monitoring system in place, he held fast to it when I returned. So it was back to the ovens and heat shield assembly for me. But it was a good deal while I had it and I even got in a little studying between strolls to check the ovens. Later in the fall with my senior year underway, financial pressures eased and I left Avco and slept at night rather than driving to Stratford for the night shift.

The second OCS increment in 1963 was heavier on leadership evaluations and the grueling hill trails hikes were steeper and longer. By then, the Corps had switched to the M14, a weapon similar to the M1 except it had a large 20 round magazine compared to the M1's eight round clip, and could be switched to fire continuously like a machine gun. We spent days on the range qualifying with the M14. My mid-level "sharpshooter" score placed me between the sneered at "marksman" and respected "expert" weapons qualification. Candidates failing to at least qualify as marksmen were viewed by DI's and company officers as subpar officer material, a distinct black mark when deciding who would successfully complete the program. Every candidate was expected to meet the Corps' "every marine is a rifleman" common denominator. None of this shooting expertise came in handy in Vietnam, but what I learned towing and marking targets for fellow officer candidates when we weren't on the firing line 200 yards up range was helpful. After a little time in the butts, we could tell by the sharp snap when a bullet passed through our target just a few feet above us, compared to shots that went through targets adjacent to us. At the time, I thought the hours hauling targets up and down, marking hits, sometimes waving a red banner known as "Maggie's drawers" if the shot went wide of the scoring area, were a complete waste of time. But three years later in Vietnam when I heard the "snap" of bullets headed our way, I knew immediately what it was and how close it was.

Aviation officer candidates faced an additional hurdle in Quantico, a day long written aviation qualification exam and a thorough flight physical. Failure to pass meant no flying and instead being a platoon leader and infantry officer or branching into some other non-flying specialty later on. The flight physical nearly ended my military flying aspirations because I couldn't keep both eyes focused on the evaluator's finger as he moved it within inches of my face. I was told to do eye exercises for the next week, practicing moving my finger toward my face to increase eye muscle strength. A week later, after much practice which drew quizzical looks from the DI's, I passed.

Flight Training

When I finished college in the summer of 1964, was commissioned and entered flight training in Pensacola, the war in Vietnam was heating up and along with it the pressing need for marine pilots, particularly helicopter pilots. And so the multi-engine pipeline became nothing more than words and pictures in a recruiting brochure. Henceforth, first tour marine aviators would fly jets or helicopters with the bulk of graduates going to helicopters. Those with the highest cumulative flight and ground school grades got their choice. The cut off occurred at Saufly Field in Pensacola at the completion of primary training in T-34B's.

As it happened, my flight grades qualified me for jets in spite of the unprecedented act (at least as far as I know) of getting airsick all over myself, and my instructor seated behind me in the aft cockpit on the first flight. Leading up to the event was an egg omelet and milk shake lunch before the flight. After climbing away from Saufly Field and leveling off around 4000 feet, the instructor, a Navy lieutenant named Morris, exaggeratedly demonstrated the function of each flight control with large, sharp, stick and rudder inputs. On that hot, humid July day, cumulus cells were building over the training area and before long, we found ourselves heading toward a billowing cell towering several thousand feet above us. Not wanting to penetrate it, Morris rolled 180 degrees, diving inverted beneath the cell, then rolled 180 degrees upright and pulled hard, zoom climbing up the cloud's back side. I recall feeling very warm. Then, without warning, my partially digested lunch explosively burst from my mouth onto the instruments, knee board, flight suit, cockpit floor and my leather flight gloves, which I inadvertently put up to my face. Morris seated in the rear cockpit, seeing and smelling what had just happened, exclaimed: "Open the canopy!" With hands covered in vomit, I grasped the canopy handle, hauling the canopy aft. Then, since there was no place not covered by vomit in my cockpit, I stuck my hands out into the airstream to blow the vomit off. The airstream stripped away some of the vomit sending it into the rear cockpit striking Morris's face and helmet visor. He said: "Aw shit, we're heading back."

National Naval Aviation Museum
A T-34B Mentor on a solo flight near Pensacola Naval Air Station.

I was silent, the vomit having clogged my boom mike. Upon landing, the "plane captain," as the enlisted lineman was called, handed me a bucket of disinfectant, sponge, and rags and I set about cleaning up my mess.

The next few hops were shaky and I thought I might not succeed, but in subsequent flights, I started to adapt to the Navy's highly structured flight procedures and I actually began to enjoy it. On solo flights, I'd do loops, rolls, and spins while my contemporaries who felt less comfortable spent solo periods flying straight and level until it was time to return. By the end of primary training, my flight grades made the cut for jets. But back in preflight ground school, a less than stellar grade on a survival test lowered my class standing and set the course for my Marine Corps flying career (a date in town the night before an exam can do that). I was destined for helicopters after completing the T-28 fixed wing syllabus, which included aerobatics, formation, instrument flying, and aircraft carrier qualification aboard the USS Lexington.

Navy T-28B and C models, with their two stage supercharged 1425 horsepower R-1820 radial engines, maximum speed of 340 knots and maximum altitude of 35,500 feet, had performance comparable to many WWII fighters. The B and C models were similar, except the C's were configured for aircraft carrier training with a retractable tailhook and shorter, wider propellers to provide deck clearance during carrier landings.

Transitioning to the T-28 was a big step from the little T-34, which instructors referred to as the "teeny weeny." Initially everything about T-28s seemed monstrous. Even starting the engine required a series of two handed well-coordinated steps. If mishandled, the cylinders would flood, sending purple 115/145 octane avgas out a cowling drain onto the ramp. Or just a few cylinders would fire and the rest of the avgas would torch out exhaust stacks, sending flames billowing over the wing.

During starts, a lineman stood by with a large wheeled fire bottle at the ready. He'd give the "all clear" signal to start and with the throttle slightly open and the starter button pressed, the student counted at least eight propeller blades rotating past the vertical. That step assured none of the engine's lower cylinders had filled with oil during the previous shutdown. In such event, oil filled cylinders would abruptly jam the starter motor, halting the start before major engine damage occurred. After the prop was freely spinning, the magnetos were switched to BOTH, followed quickly by depressing the primer button, which delivered avgas straight into the cylinders. At that point, the engine usually started. Still depressing the primer button, the student adjusted the throttle to stabilize the RPM between 1000 to 1200 and moved the fuel mixture control from idle cutoff to full rich. As RPM started to drop off from the overly rich fuel/ air mixture, the primer button was released and the throttle adjusted to get 1000 to 1200 RPM. Simple as that!

Like the T-34 training we just completed, the T-28's transition and aerobatics syllabus required competence in spin recovery and we were expected to accomplish aerobatics during solo flights. Instructors emphasized that the T-28 was a different animal from the forgiving T-34, which could always be counted on to recover in spite of a student's awkward and sometimes ill-timed stick and rudder inputs. Spin recovery was initiated after one and a half turns by simultaneously positioning the stick slightly forward of neutral and pushing full opposite rudder. But the procedure might not always work, especially if the technique wasn't up to par. In such cases, students were instructed to bail out rather than continue recovery attempts as the plane plummeted to earth. With no ejection seat, jumping clear of

2nd Lt Reiner at Whiting Field, Milton, Florida, fall of 1964, where students flew T-28Bs in Navy Training Squadron Three, mastering two and four plane formation flying. T-28s were a big step up from the much smaller T-34s and with its large 1425 horse power radial engine and 340 knot maximum indicated airspeed; it had performance similar to World War Two fighters.

a spinning T-28 was no easy feat and success wasn't guaranteed, even when done properly.

We were told escape was marginal above 200 knots because air loads would hold the body against the aircraft. And we should get out sooner rather than later because escape below 5000 feet in uncontrolled flight was also marginal.

Egress technique and direction varied with the situation. In level, controlled flight, the best option was to slow as much as possible, put the flaps down which opened two more feet of space between the wing trailing edge and the tail, and egress above 1200 feet to allow time to pop the chute. Right egress was recommended to take advantage of the propeller's downward slipstream, which would theoretically propel the pilot downward with less chance of striking the tail. In a spin, egress was to the outside of the spin; diving out from the right side in a left spin and vice versa in a right spin. In an inverted spin, we were told the previous steps were unnecessary because we would be propelled clear by negative G forces upon releasing the seat belt/shoulder harness. Students were also reminded to disconnect the boom mike and earphone chords and, if appropriate, the oxygen mask, before accomplishing any of the above steps.

The Navy provided a bailout trainer to help students master the recommended technique. A yellow T-28 with its right wing clipped off sat adjacent to the flight line. In place of the wing was a trampoline-like net to catch trainees leaping from the front cockpit, which is where they flew on solo flights. The student would strap into the front cockpit, then the engine was revved up to create a large slipstream blast. At the instructor's signal, the student disconnected his helmet chords, unstrapped, and did a rolling flip onto the net, ideally landing on his back. We were told this technique was the best way to avoid getting struck by the tail and we shouldn't be concerned about hitting the wing because the slipstream would carry us beyond it. Once clear of the plane, we were to pull the D-ring of our back pack parachutes. Students only sat in the rear cockpit for instrument training flights. Rear seat egress was more direct and dicier. Instead of a rolling flip toward the wing, the NATOPS manual specified a forceful dive at the wing's trailing edge. We didn't practice that maneuver because I suppose a forceful dive at the trailing edge didn't require any special technique and a student in the back seat on an instrument flight wasn't expected to get into trouble with an instructor in the front cockpit.

I never heard of a solo student getting into trouble doing spins, but during my time at Whiting Field, an instructor and his hapless student were forced to bail out at the end of a basic instrument period. The instructor, bored by hundreds of flights in the front cockpit while students under the instrument "bag" in the aft cockpit went through their instrument flying patterns, arranged to rendezvous north of Whiting Field with a fellow instrument instructor to engage in a dogfight. And so, with their instrument period complete, the students were instructed to retract their instrument canopies and became back seat spectators to what followed.

The facts are murky because T-28s didn't have flight recorders. But during the dog fight, one of the T-28s entered what apparently was an accelerated yawing stall which sent the plane into a spin. The instructor was unable to recover and ordered the student to bail out. He yanked the canopy handle back to the EMERGENCY position, which fired an air bottle charge into the canopy's retraction system, sending it flying back in less than a second. Then he dived clear and popped his chute. The student dived out also, but didn't open his chute. The mangled T-28 wreckage lay spread out and roped off on the VT-3 hangar floor at Whiting Field for weeks during the investigation. Speculation was that the student was struck by the spinning aircraft, but by the time the accident board made its determination, we had moved on and never learned the final conclusions.

We put the event behind us and continued through two- and four-plane formation, night flying, radio instruments, and finally carrier qualification aboard the USS Lexington. Students called it "hitting the boat." The "Lex" was a World War II Essex-class carrier retrofitted with an angled deck and upgraded catapults. It was based in Pensacola and used solely for training students and for maintaining the qualifications of fleet carrier pilots.

U.S. Navy Photo
USS Lexington, CVT 16, in the Gulf of Mexico

Before hitting the boat, we spent hours flying field carrier landings (FCLP's) at Barren Field, a small WWII-era training facility in the farmlands about midway between Pensacola and Mobile. Runway markings at Barren duplicated a carrier deck, complete with an aircraft carrier's Fresnel lens landing light system, positioned left of the runway which projected a ball of light known as the "meatball." The object was to keep the meatball in line with a row of horizontal green lights which defined the correct approach angle. Landing pattern altitude was 325 feet, airspeed exactly 82 knots, no faster or slower. Configuration: canopy open, speed brake extended, full flaps, gear down, cowl flaps open, propeller maximum increase RPM.

After 13 FCLP periods at Barren, I was in a four plane flight of students flying solo, trailed by an instructor, heading into the Gulf of Mexico to rendezvous with the Lexington about 20 miles out at sea. The Lexington appeared on the horizon like a postage stamp. Hitting the boat in the T-28 was the end of an era. Jets fly right down to the deck at approach power. In contrast, like navy WWII fighter and bomber pilots, T-28 pilots got a "cut" signal from the LSO approaching the deck rounddown. At that point the throttle

National Naval Aviation Museum

T-28C Trojan landing on the USS Lexington.

was snapped to idle and a few seconds later, the main gear thumped down on the deck and the tailhook snagged an arresting cable. After stopping, we were signaled to raise the tailhook, retract the speedbrake, and taxi forward a short distance to line up on the straight deck. Then like our WWII forbears, we'd run up the engine to assure normal operation, and, at the deck officer's signal, apply takeoff power, release the brakes, and go barreling toward the bow. Approaching the forward elevator, the student rotated to the takeoff attitude and moments later the T-28 shot past the bow, climbing away with blue water beneath its wings.

With carrier qualifications complete, we climbed several thousand feet over the Gulf, joining up with the orbiting formation of completed students, then headed north to Saufly Field. It was the last fixed wing flying we'd do in the Training Command. Next stop was Ellyson Field on the northern outskirts of Pensacola for helicopter training and from then on, that's what we would fly.

I think I can speak for all marine and navy pilots of my era about the early frustrations and exasperations of helicopter training. After "hitting the boat" in the T-28, we thought we were pretty hot studs, but the tiny TH-13M helicopter was The Great Deflator. The first few flights in that 200 horsepower machine with its plexiglas bubble-enclosed bench seat cockpit, trussed tubular tail structure, and 87 knot top speed, were a most ego shattering experience.

Rotorcraft aerodynamics and systems classes preceded the flying and defined how different the erector set contraption we were soon to fly differed from airplanes. We learned a new vocabulary of limitations like "retreating blade stall," which caused helicopters flown too fast to pitch up and roll inverted, and "dead man's curve," the dangerous low speed, low altitude combination where a safe landing after a power failure is impossible. Unlike an airplane's wings and tail that provide lift and stability, those functions in the TH-13 were derived from the main rotor and tail rotor, except for stability which was provided by the pilot. The pilot's smooth, continuous, precise cyclic stick and collective pitch lever inputs, together with the twist grip throttle and tail rotor pitch control pedals, were what kept the whole shebang under control. In short, the TH-13M had no stability and, if left unattended even for a short time, would diverge unpredictably and tumble from the sky.

National Naval Aviation Museum

TH-13 at Ellyson Field, Pensacola.

Even the preflight inspection was different. Along with the obvious look at the main rotor and tail rotor, it focused heavily on push rods, dampers, control cables, pulleys, gear box reservoir fluid levels and drive shaft linkages. The failure of any of these parts could seriously compromise control and bring the helicopter down like a hurled toy.

And then came the flying. Most of the training in that little machine was done within 500 feet of the ground at large, flat open-field sites a few miles west of Ellyson Field. On the first flight, the instructor did the departure and climb out on course to the training area, then we took control for the first time in level cruise flight. The instructor took over again for the approach and landing, bringing the TH-13 down effortlessly to a smooth hover and landing in the middle of a large white square on the grassy training field, a maneuver impossible at that point for even the most adept student.

Then it was our turn. With the instructor, alert for what was about to happen and following lightly on the controls, we made our first liftoff to a hover. And true to form, with no ingrained control habits, everything went haywire at once. When I raised the collective pitch lever, the helicopter lifted off the grass but then the rotor RPM decayed because the twist grip throttle hadn't been turned slightly to increase power and the helicopter began to turn because of the change in rotor torque. With the throttle increased the helicopter turned the opposite way. A stab on the anti-torque pedal fixed that but with the collective pitch lever ignored for the moment, we were now about 20 feet in the air and drifting off the square. Moving the cycling control to arrest the drift caused a sharp bank and drift reversal, sending the helicopter careening off the square and toward another lurching machine at an adjacent square about 500 feet away. The instructor took over and with almost imperceptible control inputs, the wild contraption became instantly stable and serene.

So it went as we gradually morphed into helicopter pilots. After 30 hours in the little machine, it was on to the CH-34, the Navy and Marine Corps main line medium helicopter. More transition flying in the CH-34 was followed by helicopter radio instrument training. And then it was over.

With 253 hours logged in 13 months, I was designated a Naval Aviator qualified in airplanes and helicopters on August 25, 1965. Nine months later, I would be flying ashore halfway around the world to a spartan beachside base outside Da Nang, South Vietnam.

National Naval Aviation Museum

UH-34 at Ellyson Field, Pensacola.

Checking into HMM-265 and Training

When I joined HMM-265 in September '65, the squadron had recently returned from a Caribbean cruise and I was among the last pilots to join the squadron prior to its WESTPAC deployment in April 1966.

The training regimen followed standard Navy doctrine. First CH-46 systems ground school for a week followed by a flight syllabus covering all missions the aircraft might be expected to perform.

Right off the bat, the normally simple act of taxiing was an unexpected and surprising challenge. Because of the helicopter's tandem rotor configuration, taxiing required a deft combination of cyclic and collective inputs sometimes coupled with differential braking. Too much cyclic input caused the rotors to pound their mechanical droop stops and like a recalcitrant horse, the helicopter would simply not respond. It was an art that took some practice to master. Then came hovering and maneuvering the helicopter several feet above the ground forwards, backwards, and sideways over squares painted on the tarmac. Following that, turns, climbs and descents were introduced. When competent with those maneuvers, flight with stabilization off, simulated engine failures, autorotations to a power-on wave off, external loads, formation and tactical formation was mastered. Full autorotations were not practiced because a less than perfect recovery could result in a hard landing, with structural damage and even failure and partial separation of the aft fuselage, which housed the aft rotor system, transmission and twin engines.

The CH-46A was a militarized and somewhat beefed-up version of the Boeing-Vertol 107 civilian helicopter which wasn't designed for the stresses of military flying and its mechanical shortcomings would become apparent in the years ahead. Eventually its flaws would be corrected through structural and mechanical modifications, but the learning curve was deadly.

Like all helicopters of its day, and most today as well, the CH-46 was dynamically and statically unstable. If not controlled by the pilot or an automatic flight control system, it would quickly deviate unpredictably from its flight path, pitching, yawing, and rolling with no tendency to return to stable flight. To ease pilot workload, the CH-46 had a dual stabilization augmentation system (SAS) which sensed pitch, roll and yaw and made control inputs to return the helicopter toward its original trimmed attitude. An additional automatic trim system and altitude hold system worked in conjunction with the SAS and maintained the helicopter's airspeed, pitch and roll attitude as well as altitude, much like an airplane's basic autopilot. These systems also made the CH-46 a passable instrument flying aircraft. With the SAS switched off or otherwise rendered inoperative, the helicopter was still controllable in the hands of a skilled pilot making smooth and rapid yaw pedal and cyclic stick inputs to maintain control. But with SAS off and left to its own without competent pilot intervention, the helicopter would quickly diverge unpredictably and tumble to earth. In any case, and in summary, when it came to flying the CH-46, pilots had to be competent, hands-on "stick and rudder" aviators to accomplish their mission and, in the extreme, to survive.

Although the CH-46 could be operated by one pilot, an aircraft commander, copilot and an enlisted crew chief were the standard non-tactical crew complement. Decked out for combat, two enlisted men, a crew chief / gunner and an additional gunner manned the passenger cabin. Their inflight training included gunnery, firing a 7.62 mm M-60 machine gun mounted in an open hatch at old metal containers and other discarded equipment. The weapons range was near the North Carolina Intracoastal Waterway adjacent to the New River Air Station. We'd fly by the containers at about 80 knots and the gunners practiced leading the targets with bursts of machine gun fire. Pilots even got to take turns firing from the passenger cabin, more for kicks than anything else. It was a fun exercise but turned out to be not very useful. In Vietnam we quickly learned that, as one would expect, the Viet Cong fired from concealed positions. Approaching or departing a landing zone, we could sometimes hear the subtle "snap" of a round passing close by or the thunk when it struck the helicopter, but locating the source of the incoming fire was another matter. In such circumstances, crew chiefs and gunners firing M-60 or .50 caliber machine guns used their instincts to "hose" an area, sending a stream of tracers in the general direction of the concealed enemy.

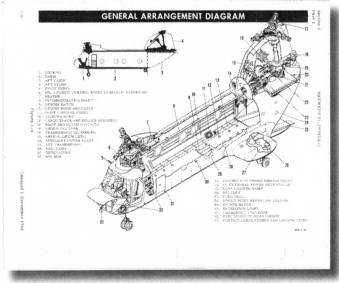

GENERAL ARRANGEMENT DIAGRAM

NATOPS Flight Manual

CH-46A General Arrangement at time of deployment.

Helicopter Nicknames
and the Painful Learning Curve

The CH-46A Sea Knight is what the Navy called it. It had just been introduced to the Marine Corps the previous year, the first arriving in my squadron, HMM-265 at MCAS New River. Nobody called it a Sea Knight and it hadn't yet been tagged with the nickname "Phrog." Why that name? I suppose because its nose-up stance and aft fuselage stub wing tanks gave it the appearance of a frog about to leap. That nickname came years after I left the Marines. During my time in the Marines, in response to the question: What do you fly? ...the answer was simply "forty-sixes." And pilots who flew the older radial engine CH-34s said they flew "thirty-fours." The only helicopters that had nicknames back then were the UH-1 "Huey," and the monstrous twin radial engine CH-37 known as "the Deuce." As in I'm a "deuce driver." In HMM-265, we were "forty-six drivers."

Like so many military aircraft before it, the CH-46 went through a series of design evolutions to increase reliability, payload, and mission capability. In keeping with military practice, each modification upgrade was assigned a sequential letter in the alphabet. Since our squadron's CH-46A's were the first helicopters out of the box, we would set the early angle of a painful learning curve. In its first few years in the fleet, the CH-46's mechanical failures and fatal accidents raised concerns up and down the chain of command, from marines in flight training aware that they would likely be assigned to CH-46 squadrons, to the highest

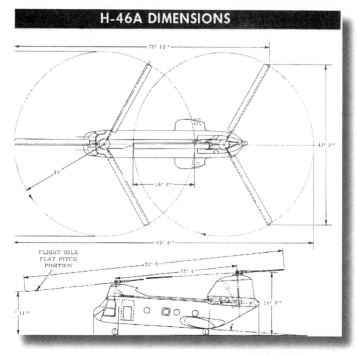

H-46A DIMENSIONS

levels of the Marine Corps, and into the halls of Congress. From 1966 through 1968, a total of 286 Marine Corps CH-46s were involved in accidents not directly related to enemy action, most of them in Vietnam.

Twenty-six were either destroyed or involved fatalities or both. Congressional investigators were appointed to determine what was wrong with the aircraft and how pilots felt about flying it. There were anecdotal reports from the training command that flight students were quitting over fears of being assigned to CH-46 squadrons. Over time, the

HMM-265 CH-46A lifting off from the Phu Bai hot point refueling area. To prevent foreign object damage and minimize compressor section erosion from sand, engine intakes had large mesh barrier filters. If the filters got clogged during a mission as indicated by high exhaust gas temperature and loss of power, the crew chief could pull a release line in the cabin which peeled open a flap on the side of the filter allowing unrestricted and unfiltered airflow to the engines. Armor plate shielding aft of the barrier filters protected the engines from small arms fire.

flaws were corrected and eventually the CH-46 was among the longest serving aircraft in the Navy and Marine Corps, having been in service over 49 years!

The Jacksonville VFW

I lived on base in the bachelors officers' quarters, taking most meals at the nearby officers' club. Off duty time at the Marine Corps Air Facility in Jacksonville, NC didn't offer much. The downtown core, dominated by pawn shops and bars, catered mainly to the needs and desires of the thousands of young marines based at nearby Camp Lejeune, home of the Second Marine Division and a few miles down highway 17, the New River Marine Corps Air Facility.

I hadn't been in HMM-265 long before I ran into RT, a tall lanky second lieutenant from Pennsylvania. Unlike me, who went through the summer platoon leader class officer program at Quantico and was commissioned directly after graduating college, RT had been around the block in the Marine Corps before arriving at the squadron.

His first contact with the military was as a one-year midshipman stint at the Naval Academy, then three years as an enlisted marine, including an overseas tour in Okinawa. He joined the officer ranks through the Marine Corps Aviation Cadet program and was commissioned when he got his wings. Some people seem almost born into the Marine Corps mold. They don't swagger or strut, it's just what they are, how they live, and what they do from one duty assignment to the next to the seeming exclusion of other interests except for the pursuit of women. RT was one of those. The Marine Corps and women, wherever he was, that was what RT was about. And he would sometimes throw caution to the winds to pursue the latter.

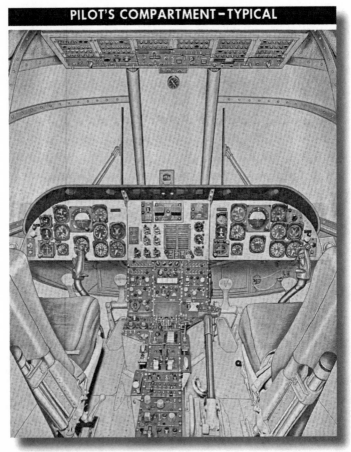

PILOT'S COMPARTMENT – TYPICAL

NATOPS Flight Manual

CH-46A cockpit layout.

One night with nothing more entertaining to do, I tagged along into town with RT. On the way he said he wanted to stop off at a place before hitting the strip. We pulled up at a frame building near the downtown that might have been a private home at one time or perhaps a shop. There was no sign outside that I could see in the darkness and without RT saying a word, we got out of the car and walked in. In the large, dimly lit room, about six or seven older men in jeans and workman-like shirts were seated at a few bare tables, smoking, drinking beers from bottles and chatting quietly. An unattended bar and five or six stools spanned one side of the room and off in an opposite corner, a black and white TV on a table was tuned to a ball game with the sound turned down. It was the Jacksonville VFW.

The cockpit of an in-country CH-46A. Note the armored seat and plastic covered collective pitch lever. Plastic covers were tried for a time to prevent the fine sand of Vietnam's coastal plain from damaging components inside the collective pitch lever. The practice was later discontinued.

The men appeared gaunt and worn like folks who spent most of their life outdoors at hard work and looked to be in their late 40's or early 50's. They all seemed to know RT and when we pulled up a chair and sat down, they greeted him casually. "How ya doing, lieutenant?" one said. From their look and bearing they were ex-enlisted. And RT seemed right at home. One of the men said, "We was just talking about how it was on Iwo." It struck me that these men, smoking and sipping beer together were frozen in time. The battle of Iwo Jima 20 years earlier was among the fiercest in Marine Corps history. The landing force suffered 6821 killed and over 26,000 total casualties. The Japanese had 21,570 killed and only 216 captured. These men, sitting, chatting, sipping beers and smoking had come through it all but somehow never left that time. They came to be among fellow war vets, to have a beer and a smoke in the low light of the VFW house. Years later, I'd see veterans at VA hospitals and military bases from the war I was soon to see, defined by that experience. And like those vets, I find myself measuring life, what's important and what's not, against the yardstick of that time.

First Casualty

E mbarkation day at MCAS New River was almost anticlimactic but by the end of the day, there was a sad surprise. Gear had already been positioned in the aircraft and all we had to do was climb aboard, crank up, check in on the common FM frequency, and prepare to launch. We had no idea that the squadron's first casualty had already occurred in our midst. But the weather was good and we departed New River in four ship sections heading north over the North Carolina countryside, then the Great Dismal Swamp of Virginia, and onward to the Norfolk Naval Base and a landing aboard the USS Boxer, LPH 4, which was tied up at pier side. We shut down and took our sea bags below to officers' country. Junior officers were assigned a large multi-bunk bay just aft of the bow and below the flight deck commonly known as the "zoo."

My first inkling of an unusual event occurred when I saw a squadron major carry a lieutenant's sea bag topside to be returned to New River. The lieutenant, a fellow pilot, was a quiet unassuming fellow who was married and had at least

U.S. Navy Photo, 1966
The USS Boxer, LPH 4, at pier side next to the carrier USS America CVA 66, Norfolk Naval Operating Base.

one small child. He had informed the squadron's commanding officer that he couldn't deploy with the squadron. We never knew why and he never rejoined the squadron and we never learned what happened to him.

One never knows what's going on in another's head. The lieutenant never let on that he had any particular difficulty or anxiety about deploying. Later, I would observe other avoidance mechanisms in dealing with combat flying, some direct, others more subtle, like always having administrative chores. A few were simply ill-suited to flying and wonked about squadron spaces, tending to the minutia of paperwork details and reports. And it was best for everyone if they stayed on the ground. Over time, everyone knew who flew the missions and who had more difficulty coping and did what they could in their own way, perhaps even subconsciously, to avoid climbing into a cockpit. Most pilots just flew their missions. But I never faulted those who hung back. I just accepted that they had defined themselves or had reached some sort of internal limit and couldn't move beyond it. Nevertheless, they were a drag on the squadron because others flew missions in their place.

The Voyage and a Chat at the Bow

Crossing the Atlantic, the squadron conducted gunnery practice. It served the dual purpose of training gunners and crew chiefs, as well giving pilots a little flight time on the month-long voyage to Vietnam. Smoke markers were dropped several miles ahead of the ship's course and pilots flew race track patterns oriented on the markers while crew chiefs and gunners got the hang of trying to hit a stationary target from a moving helicopter. Since the carrier was in a major sea lane to the Mediterranean, merchant ships occasionally steamed near us and we'd stop shooting until they passed. Then, if necessary, we'd drop more markers and resume gunnery practice.

But, for the most part, there wasn't much to do and on sunny days, the junior officers sometimes congregated at the bow beneath the flight deck to take in the sun and exchange scuttlebutt. In the ship's earlier incarnation as a World War II-era Essex Class attack carrier, two twin 40 MM Bofors antiaircraft guns were mounted beneath the flight deck to take on frontal attacks. After the war, the guns were removed, leaving the deck uncluttered and perfect for lounging about. The bow was away from the blower and machinery noises, common an aircraft carriers, and we made the most of its relative tranquility, sitting and chatting like cruise line tourists.

After a brief stop in Rota, Spain to replace contaminated JP-5, the ship continued east across the Mediterranean through the Suez Canal, stopped briefly to refuel in Aden,

Yemen, then plied east into the Arabian Sea, south through the Strait of Malacca and north to the South China Sea.

One day, while heading east in the Arabian Sea, a fellow pilot and I were out at the bow, sunning and watching flying fish break water and skim just above the waves. He came from a hard-scrabble family in Baltimore and completed two years of college before dropping out and qualifying for flight training through the Marine Aviation Cadet program. By nature, he was a cynic about life and the world in general. The Marine Corps was his vehicle for clawing up the socioeconomic scale and, unlike those who joined up to fly, this lieutenant had significant trepidation about flying. His goal then and later was, above all, survival. I found this dreary outlook amusing, but it hung like a weight on his vision of life.

So, as we sat at the bow with our faces to the warm breeze, he related a lesson of warfare survival from his readings of Rogers' Rangers, the guerilla fighters from the French and Indian War. Roger preached: "Don't go out the way you came in and don't go in the same way twice." It seemed like good advice and I resolved to remember those words. Later in my experience, I found that as axiomatic as that advice was, it often could not be applied. But not heeding it would nearly get me killed on two occasions. Then, he went on and said, "You know Arnie, you're a nice guy, but if it ever comes down to you and me, I can tell you right now it's going to be me." None of this gung-ho, "everything for my buddy" stuff for this lieutenant. For him, it was simply survival. And, thankfully, it never came down to a situation where it was either him or me.

Coming Ashore

On May 22, 1966, the Boxer arrived off the Da Nang coast and HMM 265's helicopters flew ashore loaded internally with our gear and also hauling gear externally in cargo nets. Marble Mountain Air Facility was a collection of hooches and somewhat larger corrugated metal clad structures adjacent to a linked metal Marsden matted runway. Initially, the ready room and administrative spaces were tents straddling the Marsden matted apron. The mess hall, base administrative facilities, and living areas were north of the runway. The officers billeting and our club, such as it was, were the furthest north structures on the base. Sand bagged bunkers ringed the base and beyond them were rows of concertina wire laced with claymore mines. And since the base was literally on the beach by the South China Sea, sand was everywhere.

Marble Mountain and MAG 16 Heads

From the very first day on active duty, marines learn that personal privacy is often in short supply. From barracks

HMM-265's maintenance line at Marble Mountain Air Facility in the spring of 1966. Fine grained white sand on the coastal plain throughout the I Corps area and at Marble Mountain contributed greatly to helicopter component wear, particularly to rotor blades and the small compressor blades in the CH-46's T-58 engines.

The four-holer heads in officers' country at Marble Mountain Air Facility in May 1966. When the flaps were up sea breezes generally cleared the air. Occupants passed around the latest Stars and Stripes or whatever reading material happened to be around. Two wheeled "water buffalo" trailers were positioned around the base to provide potable drinking water and for hand washing and basic hygiene.

billeting to field exercises, the Marine Corps is a communal experience and no place was this truer than the heads throughout I Corps helicopter bases from Khe Ha in the south to Marble Mountain, Phu Bai, and Dong Ha and Khe Sanh up near the DMZ.

The common head arrangement on base was a communal "four holer," a screened in shack, with plywood halfway up the sides and a flat, corrugated metal roof extending a foot or so beyond the walls and top hinged shutters, which could be lowered to keep driving monsoon rains out. There were no toilet seats per se, just a bench with cut out circles about 10 inches in diameter, two on each side. Next to the holes were a few rolls of toilet paper and often a discarded issue of Stars and Stripes, the military newspaper distributed to in-country troops. When fully occupied, four marines sat shoulder to shoulder, two by two, facing each other, clearing their bowels. It was common practice to share sections of whatever reading material happened to be around. On breezy days with the flaps up, it really wasn't bad.

Beneath the seat cut-outs, sawed off 55-gallon metal fuel drums collected the excrement. On a daily basis at Marble Mountain, the drums were switched out by Vietnamese workers via a hinged, plywood flap on the outside of the head. The workers had no regard for anyone who happened to be seated inside. They'd simply raise the flap, snatch out the full metal drum and slam in an empty one. Then they'd drag the full drum about 20 feet to an open area, pour in JP-4 and ignite it, burning out its contents. At bases further north where no hired Vietnamese workers were about, marines tended to these chores or the heads were positioned above holes dug for that purpose.

The Pilots and Off Time

With the exception of squadron department heads who were majors in their late thirties or early forties, the junior officers, that is the lieutenants and captains, were mostly in their mid to late twenties. Like me, many newly commissioned pilots from the PLC program skipped the six-month grunt oriented Marine Basic School in Quantico and went straight to flight training after graduation. A few squadron pilots with two years of college and perhaps some time as enlisted marines were commissioned through the cadet program and tended to be a bit younger for their time in rank than the average.

The Marble Mountain officers' hard back tent hooches, May 1966. Fighting holes and sand bagged bunkers straddled the hooches.

Young ladies from Da Nang in their flowing ao dais dresses arrived at the base in the afternoon to work at the officers' club serving drinks throughout the evening.

Pilots in their off time didn't stray far from their emotional set points. And since, generally speaking, the Marine Corps selects the more aggressive, action-oriented in the population, the after-hours behavior reflected these traits and was sometimes lively. Pilots prone to acting out tended to hang together, get intoxicated together, and sometimes physically confront each other. And because alcohol was cheap and flowed freely, as a hedge against fratricide, weapons were not permitted inside the officer's club.

The Marble Mountain officers' club was a screened-in hooch about 50 by 75 feet with a large bar on one side and tables and chairs covering the rest of the space. It was the only place to congregate in the evening. Our billeting hooches and the officers' club had electrical power from large four wheeled generators that powered the base but hooches were only suitable for sleeping and storing personal gear. So at

Marble Mountain hooch maids taking their lunch break. Maids lived in Da Nang and were paid by officers in each hooch to clean and do laundry. They worked Monday through Friday, arriving early in the morning and leaving around three in the afternoon.

night it was the club or nowhere. Petite, young barmaids from Da Nang worked the club, serving drinks and moving breeze-like among us in their ao dais, the traditional long, flowing dresses worn by young Vietnamese women. Early in our tour, around the first few weeks in-country, there were no specific requirements for any particular number of pilots to remain sober after a normal day's flying or office duty. But that changed one evening after pilots were unexpectedly assigned a multi aircraft mission which could only be launched after rousting a number of them out of the club. Nobody got hurt that night, but the disjointed gaggle in the night sky was a wakeup call and after that pilots, gunners and crew chiefs were always assigned night standby duty. There was no grousing about being assigned night standby duty because nobody wanted a drunken crew on dicey missions, which could be anything from a medevac to a retraction of troops in some dire predicament.

A lieutenant in our hooch was among the most volatile. He drank hard at the club, stayed late, and emerged wild-eyed and scrappy, careening in the sand outside the hooches. Sometimes he had altercations with drinking buddies and had the bruises to show for it the next day. Occasionally, unsuspecting officers venturing out at night to the urinals (screened over rocket container tubes pounded into the sand), would be harassed by the boisterous lieutenant and his drinking friends as they loudly staggered about. The scrappy lieutenant was a former MARCAD with the brains and tenacity to make it through the cadet program, but the temperament of a teenager. In quick succession, he catapulted through flight training, commissioning, marriage, the birth of a child and deployment to Vietnam. For the young lieutenant, keeping these responsibilities in alignment exceeded his ability. So, the confluence of detachment from family, stresses of combat, youthfulness, and plenty of alcohol at the club, fueled an aggressive behavior that sometimes crossed the line of physical assault. Occasionally, he would stagger back to the

By 1967, Marble Mountain Air Facility's roads were mostly paved and corrugated metal roofs replaced the tents.

Marble Mountain Air Facility (far right center) abutted the South China Sea. Da Nang airfield is at the right center north of the Cau Do River which runs toward the highlands in the foreground.

hooch, beer can in hand, bruised and bleary-eyed, collapsing on his cot and dropping the can to spill on letters from home which lay scattered about his cot. Yet, the next morning he was up for chow and headed to the squadron operations tent on the flight line like the rest of us.

In-country marines were allocated two rest and recreation (R&R) trips per tour. Venues were mostly the nearby Pacific Rim cities of Bangkok, Taipei, Kuala Lumpur, and Hong Kong, but some marines got as far as Australia and Hawaii. Arriving troops at the Asian cities were confronted by packs of bar and club representatives hawking their establishments and the beautiful and responsive ladies to be had there. Once committed for a fee, the ladies often lived with servicemen in their hotel rooms for the duration of their R & R. Some less sophisticated and needy troops became emotionally attached and at the end of their R&R, tearful farewells were a sight to behold as the troops boarded buses for the ride to the airport. Sometimes addresses were exchanged, but distance and time were corrective forces and the tenuous pay-to-play

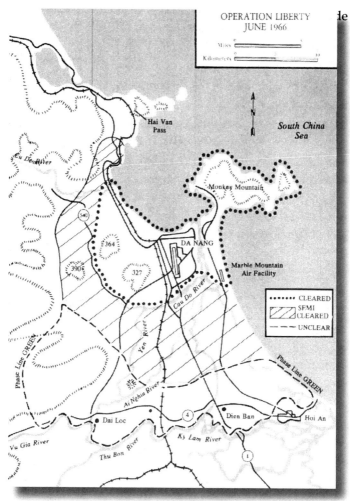

U.S. Marines in Vietnam, An Expanding War 1966 by Jack Shulimson
History and Museums Division Headquarters USMC Washington, D.C.

The Da Nang tactical area of responsibility (TAOR) in June 1966 shortly after HMM-265 flew ashore. Only the immediate vicinity of Da Nang, the Da Nang Air Base, Marble Mountain Air Facility and Monkey Mountain were considered "cleared."

bonds in place. And for the women, well the next R&R busload of primed-for-action servicemen would soon arrive from the airport. But letter romances did sometimes occur. A pilot in our hooch corresponded with a lady in Bangkok for some time.

Earlier, still weeks from flying ashore in Vietnam, a ready room briefing for lieutenants and captains was given by a major with long experience on extended overseas deployments. A memorable remark was: "Some of us won't make it back and what happens on this deployment (meaning R&R, and other random encounters outside of official duties) stays on this deployment." It was sound advice and, for the most part, stateside marriages and relationships were spared becoming casualties from this aspect of the war.

Honolulu was a prized destination among many married marines and others with committed relationships. The overnight flight from Da Nang to Honolulu for the five day R&R was also a transition to the surreal. We landed before dawn and on the bus ride along dark Honolulu streets to our hotel, I felt the sudden decompression that comes from switching quickly from war to peace. It seemed almost magically we were back in the U.S., safe, no concerns about ambushes or where to dive for cover when bullets started flying. I reveled in that bus ride.

Not surprisingly, prostitution flourished in Da Nang, although marines at Marble Mountain had limited access to their services since they rarely had transportation off the base, and when deployed to bases further north, they were on missions. But just outside the base on the road to Da Nang, small shacks with troops milling about, sometimes in lines, were a common sight. In Da Nang proper, such work was more commonly found in bars and clubs, although cruder facilities were commonplace as well. In such settings, the local urchins would sometimes tag along with the troops and contract civilian workers, chiding, joking, and hawking in pigeon English, the special abilities of their working sisters. The thinly-thatched shacks didn't shield much of the goings-on inside and the urchins, many no older than 10 or so, would peer in through the walls mimicking the moves they saw.

During my stint in the perimeter defense company, I had access to the company jeep. One day, a squadron lieutenant, with a toilet kit of hygienic materials in hand, bummed a ride into Da Nang for the purpose of quenching his natural urges. We drove into the north part of town, down a tree lined street of run down French villas. From there, we rode a three wheeled rickshaw that dropped us off at an overgrown and abandoned narrow gage railroad line bordered by tall, tropical overgrowth. On either side of the track, thatched huts of squatter families lined the right of way. The lieutenant seemed to know his way as we walked along. Old, lean, mamasans with their lined faces and black, betel nut-stained teeth stared out at us from crude doorways. Barefoot kids, some sporting Marine Corps caps, emerged from the huts, tagging alongside. I was becoming increasingly nervous because the dense foliage and the huts provided excellent ambush cover. I had a six shot .38 caliber revolver and the lieutenant carried a .45 automatic, and between us we had perhaps 30 rounds of ammunition. In that environment, we wouldn't have stood a chance.

After walking about a hundred yards down the track, the lieutenant stopped by a hut and said, "This is the place." The youngsters milled about, laughing and pointing. About that time a sweaty American civilian contract worker emerged, tucking in his shirt and nodded a greeting. Behind him a short, busty Vietnamese girl in her late teens or early twenties emerged, smiling. "You come," she said. The lieutenant walked in, she followed and closed the door. The kids flocked to the hut's thatched walls, peering, pointing and jostling each other for the best views.

Outside the hut, I kept a vigilant eye alert for the first sign of hostile intentions, like the sudden disappearance of the locals or an unnatural quiet settling over the place. But nothing happened and within about 10 minutes the lieutenant came out, sweaty and smiling, just like the contract worker before him. Then we hastily headed out of there. Although Da Nang was technically secure, everyone knew that Viet Cong infiltration at all levels of Vietnam's society was endemic and I vowed to never again voluntarily put myself in such a potentially untenable defensive situation. Hereafter, the lieutenant would have to make other arrangements for his trips into town.

Venereal disease statistics from 1963 to 1970 pegged the rate at 261.9 per thousand troops in Vietnam, according to the Army's Office of Medical History. Marine infantry probably had a lower incidence of infection because they were in the field more.

The Mission to Dong Den Mountain

June 2, 1966. Eleven days after flying ashore from the USS Boxer, Joe Roberts and I were assigned a resupply mission to the observation post atop Dong Den Mountain, a 2847 foot summit about five miles northwest of Da Nang. The weather was perfect with mostly clear skies and light winds. We departed Marble Mountain around 0800, flew a few miles to a depot area northwest of Da Nang Airfield, and picked up several marines, rations and supplies. To determine the helicopter's hover performance at the landing elevation, I checked my 1:50,000 terrain chart and determined that we had plenty of performance since we were only taking five or so passengers and a few supplies up to the zone. And it was here that I made an error that bedevils anyone who deals in different units of measure. Terrain chart height contours showed 868 which I read as feet. In fact, the terrain charts were metric with heights in meters and the landing elevation was actually 2847 feet above sea level! The mountainous area west of Da Nang was in clear view as we departed the pick-up zone on the outskirts of Da Nang. And in something of a surreal set of circumstances, we never looked at our altimeters as we climbed swiftly toward the landing zone just a few miles to the northwest.

Being from an east coast base, we had no experience in mountain flying and how deceptively low mountains can appear, even when close by. And because we were lightly loaded and the morning air was relatively cool, the error in determining hover performance was not a factor in the events that followed. In order to land as closely as possible into the wind we requested the marines on the mountain top to pop a smoke grenade to mark the wind direction. As the copilot, I set the main gear brakes and locked the nose gear so the helicopter wouldn't roll and the nose gear wouldn't swivel upon touchdown. Our wingman, Gerry Lear, and his crew orbited above.

Joe made a circuit above the zone, then lined up on the red smoke billowing from the grenade in the middle of the leveled off mountain top. The landing area was tight with just a few feet of space on either side of the main gear and not much room in front of the nose gear. Off on one side of the flattened landing area, the ground sloped up steeply and that's where the marines had dug their defensive foxhole positions. Joe slowed the CH-46 nicely as we drew near the landing point, and then brought the helicopter to a hover a few feet above the touchdown point. And that's when our world turned upside down.

As the helicopter descended, red smoke from the marker grenade streamed in through open cockpit windows, enveloping us in a red cloud atop the 2847-foot mountain.

At that point, Joe had to make a decision; pull up blindly and climb away from the mountain or continue descending the last foot or two to land. Joe chose to descend and land. Logically, it made the most sense but it was a Hobson's choice. He was betting that the helicopter hadn't drifted off the tiny, level zone.

But in those few seconds, the helicopter had drifted a few feet right, and as the left main gear and nose gear struts compressed on the ground, there was nothing but air beneath the right main gear because the ground on that side sloped sharply away. Still enveloped in red smoke, we had no sense that the helicopter had tipped sharply right until my helmet smashed against the window frame and the mountain side was just inches away, pressed against my cockpit side window. The helicopter had rolled off the flattened mountain top and lay inverted, hung up on tree stumps about 20 feet below the landing area. Fortunately, the marines had cut away trees surrounding the summit for unrestricted visibility and better fields of fire and it was those tall stumps that kept us from rolling further. When the smoke cleared, we found ourselves hanging inverted like bats, suspended by our seat belts and shoulder harnesses.

How people think and act in such circumstances would make a good psychological study. And in the seconds after the helicopter came to rest and the smoke cleared, the differences between Joe and me were marked as we hung there upside down. Fearing that the helicopter would erupt in flames at any moment, I could only think of getting out. On the other hand, Joe felt the most important thing was switching off systems such as the battery and who knows what else? I pulled the seat belt/shoulder harness release and promptly dropped across the cockpit ceiling, landing partially on Joe. I said, "Excuse me, Joe," as I made my way back into the cabin, leaving him to hang there, securing switches.

By the time I got into the passenger cabin, the passengers and our crew chief and gunner had crawled out. The right M-60 machine gun had dropped from its mount, leaving the hatch clear. There was about a foot or so clearance between the hatch and the mountainside, just enough to crawl out. About this time, Joe made his way into the cabin and I motioned to him that this was the best way out. He went through the hatch first and I followed. We crawled up about 20 feet onto the flattened landing area. The helicopter lay below us, inverted with its three landing gear poking up in the air. Several gashes were torn in the fuselage belly, most likely inflicted from tree stumps below the landing zone. The only sound was the engine's compressors spooling down.

Our CH-46 wingman, circling above us, observed the whole rollover event. They transmitted back to the base that we had crashed. After a few minutes, we all assembled at the marine's dug-in emplacement area. Miraculously, nobody was injured among our several passengers, the crew chief and the gunner. Joe Roberts, the HAC, ever the professional, just squatted there above the landing zone, peering down at the inverted helicopter making notes about what had just happened. I told him, "The important thing is that nobody got hurt." He paid no attention and continued scribbling notes.

I clambered up past the foxholes to the very top of the mountain and stared out into a strikingly different world. A light breeze scented with the mountain foliage wafted over the crest. Below was a jungle valley. In the distance, Da Nang spread out around the bay, and beyond it, Monkey Mountain and the South China Sea. Considering what had just occurred, and without the din of turbine engines and rotors, it was a most tranquil and peaceful scene to behold.

Then the sound of rotors from Gerry Lear's CH-46 making its approach about a half mile out broke the spell. I clambered back down from the peak to the foxhole emplacements and waited with the rest for Gerry to touchdown. Gerry's approach and landing were flawless. The four of us, Joe, the gunner, the crew chief, and I, scrambled aboard and Gerry lifted off for the short flight to our Marble Mountain base. It was the squadron's first accident. There would be more soon.

Doc Engert, our flight surgeon, met us on the tarmac and we were promptly whisked to the base dispensary. There, we each were given a small bottle of therapeutic whiskey, which I assume the dispensary had on hand for such occurrences. Then we were examined. Other than a few bruises, none of us had any injuries, although my helmet took a good knock during the rollover and had to be replaced.

Following the accident, a squadron board convened to assess the accident's cause. The board concluded that smoke in the cockpit was a significant contributing factor but also highlighted the need for a better method of determining the maximum load for hovering out of ground effect and suggested a simple cross reference matrix of elevation and temperature. The Navy's performance information was deemed insufficiently suitable for quickly determining helicopter loads. After the accident, we were given altitude/ temperature/payload, matrix tables for a fully fueled, crewed and armed CH-46A. Using the matrix, pilots only had to note the landing zone's elevation and temperature and add the fuel burned off to the printed load to come up with a safe hover out of ground effect load for takeoff or landing. Crew chiefs were responsible for determining the weight of cargo and for the most part, they had a conservative eye, generally telling us that loads were heavier than they actually were.

Relocating Villagers South of Da Nang, a Sad Scene

On June 7th, the squadron was ordered to relocate villagers living a few miles northwest of Hoi An, a coastal fishing town about 15 miles south of Da Nang on the South China Sea. It was one of the early population clearing efforts to move villagers to secure areas while marine infantry conducted search and clear operations. About six aircraft landed at intervals near a cluster of tree shrouded thatched huts surrounded by rice paddies. We loaded up civilians, mostly women and children with their few bundled up belongings, and transported them to villages further north closer to Da Nang inside the relatively secure tactical area of responsibility (TAOR).

Looking west from the South China Sea, the China Beach recreational facility is at the bottom; the city of Da Nang and Da Nang Air Base are at the center. Dong Den Mountain, (2847 feet MSL) about five miles northwest of Da Nang (highlighted by the arrow), was occupied by marines who manned an observation post at its peak.

It was a chaotic scene, with young mothers and their small children herded about and lined up by marines in preparation for boarding, their coolie hats and small belongings flying about in rotor downwash amid the noise of rotors and turbines. Watching the distraught women trying to hang on to their belongings in the wind and dust and their little children clinging to their mothers, trying to keep up, made me tearful, an emotion invisible to the other pilot because my helmet sun visor was drawn down. They had so little in their hamlets and now were being uprooted.

Later, squads of flack-jacketed marines with M-60 machine guns, grenade launchers and M-14s would search the huts and surroundings, then move on. These lowland areas bordering the South China Sea were mostly small

The cabin of an in-country CH-46A in the summer of 1966 as the crew chief/gunner (with his foot on a tool box) and the gunner lounged between missions. At the time squadrons were transitioning from the cotton flight suit to the new green fireproof nomex flight suit, which the crew chief is wearing. M-60 machine guns are in the port and starboard hatches.

villages surrounded by rice paddies and snow white grave mounds where the locals buried their dead. The simple structures were generally surrounded by dense tree lines, but beneath the huts and among this agrarian simplicity, snaked a Viet Cong complex of interconnected tunnels and camouflaged fighting holes. Later, because of Viet Cong encounters, the area would devolve into a hellish free fire zone, allowing gunners to fire at any targets of opportunity without first receiving fire.

The job didn't take long and not a shot was fired. We climbed up to 2000 feet, the height considered relatively safe from small arms fire, and headed northeast toward Marble Mountain. The sun was getting low as we landed, taxied to the ramp, shut down, tossed our flying gear into our individual ready room tent cubbies and headed to the chow hall for the evening meal. By military standards, an uneventful day's flying.

Napalm and the Farmer

The small villages we called "vills" in the triangle defined by Da Nang in the north, the coastal fishing town of Hoa An, about 15 miles south and An Hua about 20 miles southwest of Da Nang, were hot beds of Viet Cong activity and were constantly swept by marine patrols. Thick, dense tree lines surrounded the vills and beyond them, diked rice patties spread out in all directions with burial mounds interspersed between the patties and village huts. The tangle of small rivers, creeks, tree lines, and huts made excellent cover for the VC. When patrolling marines encountered the VC, firefights would inevitably ensue. Sometimes the VC would simply melt away, retreating into tunnels or the cover of foliage; other times they'd stand their positions and fight. Mostly, marines fought it out, sweeping through the villages with the support of Huey helicopter gunships. Sometimes Marine A-4 attack jets and F-8 fighter jets would join the fray, swooping in low to drop high explosive bombs and napalm.

On this day, not far from An Hua, on the approach to a highland river valley, a marine patrol encountered unusually intense VC resistance and the decision was made to withdraw and call in close air support to cover their extraction. We landed in a shallow, flooded rice paddy near the small village and marines broke from their cover and ran toward

These small hamlets and flooded rice paddies near Phu Bai are typical of those throughout Vietnam's coastal plain. White areas are sandy grave mounds. Viet Cong fighters often had extensive interconnected tunnels beneath the simple village huts using them to hide and move about undetected and store weapons and supplies.

our CH-46. Other marines defending the zone's perimeter with grenade launchers peered out into the tree lines in the distance, ready to return fire. Fixed wing air support was on hand and a marine A-4 attack jet swooped in about 100 feet above the tree tops simultaneously pickling off two napalm bombs directly into the village. A deep, rolling orange and black fire about 100 feet high swept over the village. Juxtaposed to this scene, about a half click away in a rice paddy, a lone farmer with his water buffalo pulling a crude farming implement, continued his work, never looking up. The last of the marines came aboard through the CH-46's aft ramp. The crew chief reported that everyone was in. And we lifted off, spiraling out of the paddy with the crew chief and gunner at their respective .50 caliber machine guns, ready to fire at the sight of any muzzle flashes from tree lines. Looking

Khe Sanh's control tower in the summer of 1966 wasn't fancy but it got the job done and since more than just rain could fall from the sky, it was also heavily sandbagged.

down, the napalm fire had by then died away leaving the village smoldering and a short distance away, the farmer and his water buffalo continued to work the rice paddy.

A Quiet Day at Khe Sanh

On June 12th, Joe Roberts and I flew north to an idyllic small base in the northwest corner of Vietnam to stand by as a backup to the Air Force "Jolly Green" helicopter rescue units tasked to retrieve downed pilots in North Vietnam. The base was Khe Sanh and at the time, in June 1966, it was a sleepy fortified Special Forces outpost with a few platoons of smiling ARVN troops milling about.

We landed and shut down, leaving our crew chief and gunner waiting near the helicopter. Forested hills to the west and north arced around the base. It was lush, green, quiet and had an idyllic, dreamlike tranquility about it. The outpost's defense line consisted of narrow slit trenches and arcs of concertina barbed wire circled the base. We walked through an opening in the concertina wire past a few hard back tents into the Special Forces bunker... and waited to be called. The bunker was a sturdy place, excavated about 10 feet below ground level and able to withstand small arms fire and hits from light mortars. Dirt and sand bags were piled atop the bunker's thick mahogany beam roof which, in turn, was supported by massive squared off mahogany posts. It wasn't that the Special Forces were going "high end." Mahogany is native to Southeast Asia and it was the easiest and closest material to acquire. Inside, a few light bulbs illuminated map tables, field telephones and radio sets and the place smelled like a furniture store.

As things turned out, it was a quiet day and we weren't needed. That afternoon we flew back to Marble Mountain. Soon that sleepy outpost in the northwest

Khe Sanh in May 1966 was an outpost in transition. This view of the underground command post bunker faces northwest toward the hills which marines would soon occupy in ever greater numbers to counter the growing North Vietnamese presence. By the spring of 1967 the base had been substantially reinforced and heavy skirmishes occurred in the hills three miles northwest, culminating in the so-called "Hill Fights" in March to May1967 and the siege of Khe Sanh in 1968.

corner of South Vietnam would be among the most contentious in the war, culminating in the so called Hill Fights the following year and the siege of Khe Sanh.

Khe Sanh's entrenchments were under construction in the spring of 1966. At the time the base was tranquil but that soon changed.

Flying Backwards with Maxwell

Retrieving patrols at night was always dicey and for that reason wasn't done except in the most dire circumstances. Lifting besieged marines at night from a mountainous zone was especially demanding and dangerous. On this night, I was the copilot for Captain John Maxwell, a solid

Wash up time at Khe Sanh's command post, spring 1966.

airman with good instincts who had transitioned to helicopters after years of flying large fixed wing transports, the Navy versions of the C-54 and C-119. We were number two in a two-ship flight fragged to extract a group of marines from a highlands area about 20 miles southwest of Da Nang.

Using the patrol's best estimate grid coordinates, we plotted their distance and bearing on the ready room wall-sized map of the area which was overlaid by a compass rose atop the Da Nang airfield TACAN. With no landmarks visible at night, navigating to the coordinates using TACAN distance and bearing was the only way to accurately find one's way at night.

We lifted off from Marble Mountain, joined up in a loose left echelon formation and headed southwest using the radio magnetic indicator bearing pointer and distance display to navigate to the approximate pickup point. Rotating beacons were off and the only lights were the helicopter's red and green navigation lights and the dim formation lights.

Checking in on UHF with Landshark, the marine mission following organization, we confirmed there were no "save-a-plane" advisories affecting our course. Over heading the grid coordinates, the leader made contact with the grunts on the mountainside. The plan was that the grunts would shine a red flashlight on a safe approach path and the lead helicopter would come in on the light. It worked up to a point and the leader was able to make his approach and land with the aid of the helicopter's nose landing light.

But when our turn came to pick up the remainder of the patrol, we couldn't see the flashlight beam. Descending below the mountain peaks, which were obscured by darkness, our only guidance was the patrol leader's voice on the FM radio directing our approach. We knew we were lower than the mountain peaks because the line of sight UHF TACAN lost its signal, as indicated by the OFF flag covering the distance readout and the RMI needle slowly spinning around the compass rose instrument. Not knowing exactly how far we were from the jungle's high terrain was an unsettling, eerie sensation. The only height information came from our radio altimeter pointer oscillating between 300 and 500 feet as we crossed over the uneven terrain below.

Flying along slowly at 40 to 50 knots, John did his best, taking directions from the officer on the mountainside, but he inadvertently eased the nose up too far. Airspeed dropped off to zero and the CH-46 shuddered. With no outside references in the darkness and not wanting to fly too fast with no idea of our distance from the terrain and trees, we had inadvertently slowed to a stop and were starting to fly backward. Maxwell pulled in more collective pitch and eased the nose down stopping the rearward flight and gradually accelerated, bringing the airspeed indicator back to life and finally to around 60 knots. About then, the voice on the FM radio said we appeared to be headed toward him.

Maxwell switched on the nose searchlight, illuminating the mountainside just a few hundred yards ahead and we came in on the hillside and landed. The marines dashed on board and we lifted off, spiraling steeply above the mountain. Once above the terrain, the TACAN needle and DME locked onto Da Nang TACAN and we were on our way back to Marble Mountain with the relieved patrol safely on board.

That night everyone performed to the best of their ability but we nearly lost control and crashed. It highlighted the limitations and hazards of night operations in high terrain with the equipment in use at the time.

Stint as a Grunt

At the end of June, there was a need for a platoon commander to oversee the southern perimeter defense of the Marble Mountain base. And our skipper, colonel Mendenhall, chose me.

In those days, officers destined for flight training were not required to go through Marine Basic School in Quantico after commissioning so I had no experience as an infantry commander. Nevertheless, there I was commanding a platoon from a high ground bunker overlooking the southern perimeter of bunkers, concertina wire, and claymore mines, which was all that kept the VC from overrunning the base from that direction. What went into the old man's decision, I can't say, but junior officers were periodically plucked from squadron flying duties for various tasks. The worst job was forward air controller (FAC) assignments, which meant that they would be out in the field with the grunts, coordinating air support missions. Thankfully, that never fell to me.

My log book shows that from time to time I did some flying, but mostly I oversaw my platoon of enlisted men with the assistance of a staff sergeant. At night, the marines kept watch and tried to stay awake in shifts and during the day, they maintained the perimeter and checked the concertina wire and claymore mines out in front of their partially buried, sandbagged bunkers. During this time, we were never confronted by the VC and nights out on the sand dunes staring into the darkness toward Marble Mountain off in the distance was just a boring ritual.

After my month long hitch as the Marble Mountain southern defense perimeter platoon commander, Lynn La Pointe, another junior pilot in the squadron, took over the platoon and shortly after that, things perked up. My job was to check him out on the normal routines of his duties, the phone communications with each sand bagged bunker behind the barbed wire defensive perimeter, the daily patrols beyond the wire to inspect claymore mines placed beyond the bunkers and between the concertina barbed wire rows, introduce him to the platoon staff sergeant, and give him a tour of perimeter's defenses.

On my last night on the perimeter, Lynn and I sat in beach chairs outside the command bunker high on a dune about 75 yards behind the main defensive positions watching the flares out to the west cascading south of Da Nang Air Base. I had just mentioned to Lynn that the number of flares seemed about what we always saw and it was looking like a quiet, routine night. No sooner than I said that, the muffled "thunks" of outgoing mortar rounds reached us from the swamps south of the Da Nang Base. Seconds later, the sound of automatic weapons fire came from the same area. Then exploding mortar rounds enveloped the perimeter. Exploding mortar shells have a distinct sound. Unlike the sharp snap of a bullet, or the echoing "thunk" of a mortar round, which is similar to large fireworks as the projectiles leave the tube, a detonating round seems to last a few milliseconds longer, almost like hearing the individual grains exploding in their turn.

We leaped through the sand-bagged bunker entrance. Although it was too dark to see the perimeter, I could hear the incoming rounds detonating in no particular pattern all around us.

Lynn didn't perceive it that way. "They're aiming for our command bunker," was his stressed declaration. I didn't refute Lynn but was inwardly amused at how someone could perceive that such an unfocused barrage could be somehow aimed at our small command bunker. The barrage lasted no more than a minute, most likely because the VC had come under fire from marines south of the Da Nang base. Almost immediately after it ended, a call came over the land line that an unexploded mortar round had struck one of the perimeter bunkers. I told the marines to remain well clear of the bunker and said to Lynn that I would go down to check out the situation. Lynn, concerned that the situation was too unsettled, advised against it. I left the command bunker in Lynn's hands and headed toward the perimeter.

As I moved across the rolling dunes, a hastily assembled reinforcing platoon from inside the base headed toward us at a dead run, yelling as they came. By the sound of it, at least a few had been drinking before they were rousted out with their weapons and ordered to the base's southern perimeter. And seeing my moving silhouette against the light of distant flares, several opened fire. An orange tracer went about 30 feet wide, other shots were closer judging by the characteristic snap that I heard so often towing targets back in OCS on the Quantico weapons range. I dropped to the sand, lying as flat as I could and called out to cease fire, and to my slight surprise, they did. That night, I came very close to becoming a fratricide casualty. Lynn could be alarmist and emotional, but that night he was right.

I shouldn't have left the command bunker and instead handled the undetonated mortar round coordination over the land line phone.

Operation Hastings and Helicopter Valley

I was spared the aeronautical debacle of Operation Hastings. On July 15, 1966, the day Operation Hastings began, I stayed back overseeing the base's southern perimeter. Lieutenant Chick Fracker flew with Joe Roberts, the aircraft commander I was normally paired with. So that morning while I walked the dunes of Marble Mountain's defense perimeter checking claymore mine installations and the integrity of barbed concertina wire, my squadron mates were up north, landing marines in the unit's first multi-squadron helicopter assault about a mile south of the DMZ.

Oversights at senior planning levels got things off to a bad start. As the first waves landed, pilots heard Colonel Richard Hunt, the MAG 16 commander circling above the operation in a helicopter, exclaim on the mission frequency, words to the effect... "Three helicopters down in the zone and not a shot fired." Joe Roberts, the star-crossed HAC who a month earlier rolled our CH-46 off the top of Dong Den Mountain, got cut off by another helicopter maneuvering on short final approach and had insufficient power to arrest his descent and settled into trees. Then two CH-46s were destroyed in landing zone collisions. Another helicopter struck by ground fire lost transmission fluid and made a forced landing, shearing off its landing gear. Later that afternoon, a fifth was shot down in flames. This narrative is a distillation of ready room talk in the days following that assault, official Marine Corps chronologies, and pilot accounts in Marion Starkey's book, *Bonnie-Sue*.

Associated Press Photo

During a late afternoon resupply mission on July 15th, EP-171 from Marine Squadron HMM-265 was struck by NVA antiaircraft fire at 1500 feet. The rounds most likely passed through the un-armored belly, penetrating the engine compartment, shutting down an engine, and igniting a fuel fire which engulfed the tail section and spread forward through the fuselage interior. The pilots entered an autorotative descent, jettisoning their window hatches in order to clear the smoke and see outside. The copilot reported that they spotted the ground at low altitude, pitched up to slow their descent and struck trees as they touched down on a hillside. The helicopter rolled over and burned furiously. Twelve marine infantrymen died in the fire and the crew chief, Sergeant Robert Telfer, whose leg became entangled in the wreckage and could not be pulled free, also died. The HAC, Captain Thomas C. McAllister, and copilot First Lieutenant George, Richie, suffered burns. Mc Allister required a short hospitalization. The gunner, Sergeant, Gary Lucas, had more serious burns and was medevaced to the U. S. for treatment.

U.S. Marines in Vietnam, An Expanding War 1966 by Jack Shulimson Bonnie Sue, A Marine Helicopter Squadron in Vietnam, by Marion F. Sturkey 1996.

The mission, to destroy the 1500-man 90th North Vietnamese regiment in a mountain valley about five miles northwest of Cam Lo, was straight forward enough from a high level command perspective. But the operation's Achilles Heel was the planner's failure to accommodate adverse winds and their effect on the heavily loaded CH-46's as they maneuvered to land in the relatively small clearing known as Landing Zone Crow in Song Ngan Valley.

The unplanned-for tailwinds caused helicopters to lose lift as they maneuvered at low altitude for landing and also required a higher than normal nose high pitch in order to slow to a hover, decreasing forward visibility. This combination, coupled with the relatively small landing zone, funneled helicopters into a very constrained area setting up landing accidents in which seven marines were injured and two killed, one of whom was cut in two by flying rotor debris. Then a CH-46, hit by small arms fire near landing Zone Crow, lost transmission fluid and sheared off its landing gear during a forced landing. Later that day, a CH-46 was shot down when NVA anti-aircraft rounds ignited a raging fire in the tail section. Smoke entered the cockpit, obscuring outside vision. The pilots jettisoned their window hatches and yawed the helicopter to clear the smoke. Nearing the ground, they flared as the helicopter passed through trees on a hillside, touched down, and rolled over. Rotor blades fragmented and the helicopter burned furiously with ammunition cooking off in all directions. Thirteen marines, including the crew chief, died in the blaze. Both pilots and the gunner managed to grapple themselves out of the wreckage with burns.

By the end of the day, four helicopters had been destroyed, two from my squadron, HMM-265, and two from HMM-164 our sister squadron. A fifth, from HMM-164, the one that made the forced landing and sheared its landing gear, was later recovered. Out of the five downed helicopters, three losses were due to the confined landing area and failure to accommodate adverse winds in the landing zone. The enemy accounted for one shoot down and one forced landing. And because of group commander Colonel Hunt's on-air exclamation about crashed helicopters in the landing zone, he was thereafter often referred to around the ready room as "Chaos Five," the number five referring to his colonel's 05 rank.

After that day, the Song Ngan Valley was known in the Marine Corps and later, in newspapers and Vietnam histories, as "Helicopter Valley." The operation lasted through early August and involved about 8500 marines and 3000 ARVN fighting 8000 to 10,000 North Vietnamese regulars. The North Vietnamese, who lacked the fire power and air support of the marines and ARVN troops, came out on the short end, losing 824 killed and 17 captured, against Marine Corps losses of 128 killed, 162 wounded and 21 ARVN killed and 40 wounded.

A Memorable Trip to Da Nang

Deviating from well-developed habits, like not putting your car keys where you always do, then forgetting where you put them, can be inconvenient, but in war, it can be worse. Driving back in a jeep with Huey Walsh across the Cau Do River pontoon bridge between Da Nang and our base by the sea, we came under a hit and run attack from VC out in the swamps south of the bridge.

I pulled over and stopped and Huey and I hopped out of the jeep with our weapons drawn to return fire. ARVN soldiers at the bridge ran toward the swamp to engage the VC, but by then they had melted away into the reeds. It was at that point that I discovered my .38 revolver was unloaded. I had forgotten to reload the weapon after leaving the PX. In

A street in Da Nang, June 1966.

the past, I had never unloaded my revolver before entering
the PX (even though a sign at the door told all who entered
to do so). My view was that the sign was more intended
for marines carrying automatic weapons which were more
prone to accidentally discharge. But on this occasion, I
chose to obey the instructions. And not being in the habit of
unloading, I forgot to reload. Luckily, the VC chose to run
rather than fight.

R.T. and Joe Roman's Marble Mountain Crash

One benefit of my month long stint as a platoon commander was that I was not as exposed to the hazards of flying as those who flew every day. During that period, the first of many mechanical mishaps occurred. As time went on, CH-46 helicopters had an increasing number of mechanically related fatal accidents and aircraft groundings became common.

The first event occurred on September 14, 1966 on a morning repositioning flight from a base dispersal site to the flight line. Aircraft commander Joe Roman, copilot R.T. Harry, and crew chief corporal W.L. Diehl were on the downwind leg of their approach to the runway when one of three bolts holding the aft rotor's control yoke assembly failed, which essentially unhinged the aft rotor system's control mechanism.

The shattered wreckage of Joe Roman's and R.T. Harry's CH-46 was hauled from the surf and deposited north of the runway in what was to be an ever growing boneyard of destroyed aircraft. The accident was caused by a mechanic who failed to properly fasten a bolt on the aft rotor control yoke.

R.T. said he heard a loud bang and the helicopter pitched up, out of control. He thought the helicopter's stabilization augmentation system had malfunctioned and reached down toward the pedestal to disconnect it, but the helicopter's vibrations were so extreme that he was unable to reach it. By then, Joe Roman had lowered the collective pitch and begun a quick descent, while the helicopter continued to pitch wildly from one extreme attitude to another.

Observers on the ground watching the helicopter's erratic descent thought the pilots were just fooling around, but reality quickly set in when the helicopter kept plunging toward the surf adjacent to the runway. It struck the water in an extreme nose up attitude and the aft rotor system rotated forward, slicing the fuselage in two. Fortunately, corporal Diehl chose to sit on the cockpit's center pedestal during the short positioning flight or he would have been killed by the aft rotors slicing through the CH-46's cabin. The cockpit came to rest on its left side in several feet of surf and R.T. found himself underwater in the left seat. He extricated himself and popped to the surface to find that a fuel fire had ignited, which in turn, was cooking off the aircraft's .50 caliber machine gun ammunition. With the helicopter in just a few feet of surf, all three crewmembers were able to escape from the burning wreckage and make their way to the beach, banged up, but all things considered, not too much worse for the experience.

Still in my role of executive officer of the base defense company, I was in the command bunker when the accident occurred early that morning and missed all the excitement. Returning to the hooch that morning, I saw R.T. Harry lying on his cot bruised up. Our hooch maid, Van, had by then arrived with the other maids from Da Nang and was keeping her distance from R.T.'s cot and trying to be quiet. She pointed to R.T. when I walked up the steps and into the hooch and said, "R.T...he hurt bad."

The accident board concluded that a mechanic's failure to appropriately fasten a nut in the control yoke assembly caused it to loosen and fail. It was the first accident in a long streak of CH-46 mechanical and maintenance-related mishaps that were to come during our tour and in the next several years.

By October 1966, my hitch as executive officer of the Marble Mountain defense company had ended and I had also been transferred to HMM-164 along with Captain Art Chapman, another HMM-265 squadron mate. Such transfers were a routine part of staggering tours so that an entire squadron population didn't depart Vietnam at the same time. But Art and I were delighted to leave HMM-265, a squadron that we felt was staffed by a cadre of grumpy majors.

Children of I Corps

The children in these pictures lived mostly around Da Nang. Some were cared for at an orphanage near Marble Mountain, some lived with families, and others appeared to be street kids.

During a temporary assignment as the executive officer of the Marble Mountain defense company, I assisted in civil affairs activities at an orphanage near China Beach where marines provided food assistance

Da Nang orphanage children lining up for snacks. 1966.

and other material support. Thousands of children were orphaned during the war. After the war, children with mixed race features were sometimes abandoned by their mothers and generally ostracized by Vietnamese society.

Residents at an orphanage near Marble Mountain Air Facility, 1966. This caregiver chewed Betel nuts which stained her teeth black.

Street children.

Marines called it "Dog Patch," a shanty town of makeshift shops near the Da Nang PX, 1966.

Our helicopter crew chief sharing rations with children while the family awaited transport out of Khe Sanh, January 1967. Khe Sanh would soon devolve into one of the most hotly contested areas of the war.

Looking for Pappy and Ron

It's common for a new pilot to fly with the commanding officer at some point after joining a squadron and my time came almost immediately on a fruitless search and rescue mission. Former squadron mates William E. (Pappy) Johnson and Ron Pfeifer from HMM-265 went missing on a flight from Phu Bai to Marble Mountain on the misty night of October 6, 1966. The next day, a multi squadron search was launched for the missing helicopter EP-154, Bureau Number 151960. I took off from Marble Mountain with the CO of my new squadron, HMM-164, heading north over Da Nang Bay, then over the Hai Van Pass. This was their most likely route back from Phu Bai. Our search area was the immediate vicinity of Da Nang so the flight didn't last long. The skipper was a grey-haired, amiable fellow named Watson, whom members of the squadron nick-named "Dad" (but not to his face). He rarely flew and spent most of the time at his desk. I was briefed by other members of the squadron to only speak when spoken to during the flight. I did most of the flying and he hardly said a word other than to handle the radios and instruct me to head this way or that. It was the only time I flew with him. The multi squadron search was fruitless and was called off four days later.

There was a rumor that the wreckage had been located in the Hai Van Pass area. An MIA report later stated that Ron Pfeifer's remains had been recovered January 10, 1969 and William Johnson's remains were recovered on January 14, 1969 at grid coordinates that didn't match any Vietnam War era charts. Aside from the aircraft loss report, there was no accident report issued following the recovery of the bodies. If the rumored location was correct, we had flown over the wreckage in the jungle-canopied Hai Van Pass.

With no wreckage analysis, one can only speculate about the cause. The tragedy came at the confluence of multiple conditions. Low clouds shrouded the area and it was night. In low visibility, Marine Corps helicopter pilots, although instrument qualified, often preferred to fly using visual ground references, backed up with radio navaids, as opposed to purely radio-instrument flying using TACAN and ADF with air traffic control radar monitoring. Consequently, aircraft were sometimes flown inadvertently into unlighted or cloud shrouded terrain, an event known in aviation circles as a "controlled flight into terrain" accident. It's a common type of helicopter accident, even to this day. On the other hand, a system malfunction could have brought the helicopter down. In such circumstances, pilots commonly transmit a distress message, but helicopter mechanical malfunctions can occur so suddenly and catastrophically that a distress report might not be possible.

In January 1969, when the remains of Pappy and Ron were recovered, marines were still involved in combat operations and, in view of those priorities, it's understandable that assets would not be allocated to sift through the shattered wreckage of a helicopter that had gone down nearly three years earlier. Without an accident report, the cause will never be known.

Que Son Valley Nui Lac Son Assault

Several weeks after checking into HMM-164 in the fall of 1966, I was Jim Hollis's copilot on a multi-squadron troop insertion in the Que Son Valley south of Da Nang. Several sections from the squadron landed in an assembly area south of Hoi An where we shut down with about 20 other aircraft in the joint Vietnamese and U.S Marine operation in the fertile Que Son Valley. The mission was to land marines in an expanse of rice paddies near Nui Loc Son to confront a growing number of VC and North Vietnamese troops exploiting the bountiful rice harvest in this fertile rice growing area.

In due course, we were briefed with formation assignments and grid coordinates, troops were boarded, we started engines, engaged rotors, and lifted off. Formations joined up in a large, arcing rendezvous turn and headed for the rice paddies near Nui Loc Son. Approaching the rice paddies, the formations loosened up, allowing more space for pilots to pick touchdown spots. It was quickly obvious that our arrival was not unexpected because tall bamboo shafts were sticking out of the water all over the paddies.

Forested hills flanked the approach into the paddies and descending through about 200 feet, our helicopter took several hits from concealed enemy hillside positions. The crew chief returned fire, sending a stream of tracers into the hillside. One round struck the forward rotor head, damaging a control linkage. The round, probably from an AK-47, transmitted its energy through the linkage causing a jolt throughout the helicopter. A second round went through the cabin striking a marine in the torso. Our crew chief/gunner called over the interphone that a marine had been hit. Just ahead, helicopters were splashing down in the flooded paddies. We continued down, landing close behind the others. I lowered the aft ramp and our marines unstrapped and charged out. A corpsman accompanying the marines, stayed behind tending to the badly wounded marine. We quickly lifted off and I radioed the flight leader that we were breaking formation and heading for the nearest medevac facility which was about 25 miles north and across the road from our Marble Mountain base. Our adversaries obviously had been tipped off about the troop strike, a common occurrence on joint U.S.-Vietnamese operations.

On the way back, the corpsman did what he could for the wounded marine but the torso wound had caused massive bleeding and the marine was slipping away fast. Approaching the hospital, we checked in on FM and advised that we had a badly wounded marine on board. As soon as we touched down at the hospital pad, hospital corpsmen rushed out and took the marine off in a stretcher, with the corpsman following along.

Now we just had to lift off the hospital pad and hop across the road to our Marble Mountain base. Jim was concerned about the hit we took coming into the rice paddy and said we should both be on the controls in case we had a jam of some sort. In retrospect, had the linkage failed or jammed, we wouldn't be able to control the helicopter and it would have been a better idea to shut down and assess the damage. But that would have obstructed the hospital pad, making it difficult or impossible for other medevacs to arrive. We lifted off, the damaged linkage held, and we landed uneventfully across the road at our base.

After shutting down, we walked into the cabin and saw the hole in the fuselage where the round came in and the massive amount of blood left on the troop seat and floor by the wounded marine. The forward rotor head had impact damage to a pitch control linkage. Had it been severed, we likely would have crashed in the rice paddy. We learned from the hospital that the wounded marine we had just brought in died of his wounds.

Unsuccessful Recon Extraction and My Purple Heart

An axiom in war is to avoid repetition. Don't go out the way you came in and don't go in the same way twice. Unfortunately, there's often no alternative and in such circumstances there often are consequences, especially if the repetition isn't the route but the point over which a helicopter must hover.

Marine reconnaissance teams were routinely dropped into the forested hills northwest of Phu Bai to learn what they could about NVA Ho Chi Minh trail infiltration routes from Laos. On October 2, 1966, a four-marine recon team was confronted by an NVA force and came under attack. Jim Hollis and I were assigned the emergency extraction mission after a CH-34 attempting the extraction had been shot up and forced to leave the area. A Huey gunship provided fire suppression and an A-4 attack jet circled overhead. But the jungle was thick and the marines were concealed and unable to provide targeting instructions other than advising that the NVA were in close. We knew that already, since the CH-34 had recently departed with radios disabled from ground fire.

Jim was a fairly new aircraft commander (HAC) and didn't feel comfortable in the right seat so he asked me to fly from the HAC's right seat. It made no difference to me and helped get me comfortable flying on the right side when I moved up to HAC a few months later.

Jim spiraled down and as we slowed to hover over the small jungle clearing above the encircled marines, the NVA opened fire with automatic weapons. Perhaps it was the rotor downwash that threw their aim off or just luck, but we didn't take any hits that we were aware of. But being in a high hover and taking nearly point blank AK-47 fire was untenable, and Jim pulled in collective pitch and we flew off.

We told the gunship pilot that we had taken quite a lot of small arms fire and radioed that under the circumstances, a hoist extraction was out of the question. He radioed back that he would make a run on the NVA positions if we came back around and gave it another try. The A-4 pilot said he would make a run also. With the NVA so close to the surrounded marines, the idea didn't make much sense since the marines and NVA were concealed in the jungle with their positions only vaguely defined by smoke wafting from small arms fire. But Jim agreed and we turned back and descended toward the jungle clearing while the Huey gunship swung around and made a gun run at the suspected enemy positions. If the A-4 fired its twin 20 mm cannons, I didn't see any tracer fire or explosions. Apparently, it just made an intimidating run which was just as well since the NVA were in so close to the recon team that its 20 mm rounds could have just as easily struck the marines.

Approaching the clearing at 50 feet, there was no sign of the marines, just a grey, smoky haze wafting up from the small arms fire. Jim flew the approach and briefed me to follow lightly on the controls in case he got hit. No sooner had we pulled to a hover than the NVA cut loose with nearly point blank automatic AK-47 fire. Their muzzle blasts were so loud that I thought for a moment our gunners had opened fire. In quick succession, a round came through the nose striking Jim's rudder pedal. Another came through the floor by my collective pitch lever, splintering, striking my left elbow and destroying my wrist watch which was in my left arm pocket. The round continued into the cockpit overhead and stopped in the forward transmission housing. Another round hit a wire bundle knocking out our intercom and an AC electrical bus, illuminating the master caution panel

The heavy recoil of fast-firing M2 aircraft .50 caliber machine guns sent shudders through the CH-46.

warning and several lights on the caution panel. Jim pulled in collective and I switched the hover aft rotor head control to forward flight. Concurrent with all this, our gunners opened up with their .50 caliber machine guns spraying the jungle. The small arms fire immediately ceased. Perhaps the .50 caliber rounds had hit home or maybe the NVA dove for cover amid the heavy, close range fire coming at them.

I motioned to Jim to head for a ridgeline off to our left, thinking that if we had to make a forced landing, at least we would have the ridgeline between us and the NVA. But although holed pretty well, the helicopter wasn't seriously damaged and we flew off toward Hue, the closest secure area where there was a small landing strip. Although bleeding a little through my flight suit from shards of bullet shrapnel, I wasn't seriously injured. The bulk of the shrapnel had destroyed my wristwatch and passed into the cockpit overhead.

Now with our radios inoperative because of the bullet damaged AC electrical bus, we continued on to Hue Citadel and landed without further incident. Assessing the damage, it was clear that we had been quite fortunate not to have been shot down. A round had penetrated the stabilization augmentation system control closet behind the right cockpit bulkhead and the cockpit had several holes as well.

We left the helicopter to the squadron maintenance crew, which was flown in and we were helicoptered back to the Phu Bai airstrip where a corpsman deadened the elbow area and picked out most of the shrapnel. Thirty-five years later, an x-ray revealed several specks of shrapnel still in my left arm.

The mission was untenable. Even if we had been able to hover above the small jungle clearing, hoisting the marines out would have been impossible with the NVA so close. Amazingly, the surrounded recons held out and were rescued the next day by a company of marines sent into the area. Perhaps the stream of .50 caliber rounds sprayed out by our gunners made a difference.

I never found out where the reinforcements were landed in that hilly terrain, how they linked up, and what happened to the pursuing NVA soldiers. Most likely, with the arrival of more marines they thought better of making a fight of it and retreated back toward Laos.

Two small disk patches mark where our helicopter took nose hits during the attempted recon extraction. AK-47 rounds penetrated the stabilization control system closet behind the right cockpit seat. Another shot penetrated the cockpit floor behind the right collective pitch lever, splintering and striking my left arm. Parts of the bullet passed into the cockpit overhead, striking the forward transmission housing.

Khe Sanh's Changing Scene

As the months dragged on and the 1966 winter monsoon settled in around the northern I Corps, NVA presence along the DMZ and Quang Tri Province increased and marines responded by building outposts and fire bases just south of the DMZ. Con Thien and Gio Linh were on the coastal plain near the sea with the main Dong Ha base further south. Further west, units in the Rockpile area served as blocking forces at the base of the northern highlands. Khe Sanh was the westernmost base in the highlands and it grew progressively as the NVA threat increased with marines spreading out to strategic hilltops northwest of the base. Our support missions around Khe Sanh increased in lockstep with the buildup and that often involved deployments, usually in two ship sections from CH-46 and H-34 squadrons along with a Huey gunship element assigned to Khe Sanh for several days at a time.

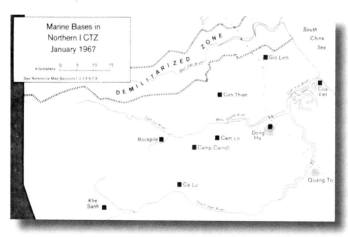

The U.S. Marines in Vietnam, Fighting the North Vietnamese 1967
Headquarters, USMC, Washington, D.C

Marines navigating their way through Khe Sanh's mud during the 1966-67 winter monsoon period.

During the early build-up, we lived in tents, ate at the mess tent, showered when we could in field showers and defecated in the standard "no-flush" field latrines positioned about the base. When they filled up, marines simply dug a new hole and moved the shack. Winter monsoon rains turned Khe Sanh's roads and pathways into brown, clinging mud quagmires with foot-deep ruts and night temperatures dipping into the low forties. We slept on cots in sleeping bags. Rats from the countryside found the marines particularly hospitable hosts or at least it seemed that way to us. Traps were everywhere but didn't seem to make a dent in the population. At night, they were everywhere and ran freely through our billeting tents. I'd go to sleep hearing their scratching claws scamper up the tent poles. What they did up there, I never thought to wonder. I just went to sleep. I never heard of anyone getting bit, but they owned the night in those cold, damp tents.

When the monsoon broke and warmer weather arrived, insects took over, but we were equipped for the swarms. Grunts carried small plastic olive drab squirt containers of repellent in their helmet bands. I carried a few in my helmet bag.

To "clear the air" in Khe Sanh tents, we had cans of aerosol insecticide. During one period in the spring, swarms of small white moths hatched and seemed to envelope the base and at night, were drawn to our tent by the lone light bulb hanging from a tent pole. A quick arcing aerosol burst caused them to drop like snow. We breathed so much aerosol mist in the tent's stagnant air that we probably could have cleared the moths with our breath.

Marines returning from perimeter patrol at Khe Sanh, March 1967. Twin-engine, Air Force ("Ranch Hand") C-123 transports like this were equipped with defoliant spray rigs and frequently landed at the Khe Sanh base. Agent Orange was sprayed extensively in Vietnam and Laos to expose NVA jungle supply routes and staging areas.

Cleared areas mark marine blocking positions in the valley between the Rockpile and the razorback ridgeline in the early months of 1967.

With the passing of the winter '66 monsoons, the DMZ area became increasingly contentious. Pilots weren't given any big picture intelligence briefings about large NVA movements, but more frequent deployments from Marble Mountain north to Dong Ha and Khe Sanh and increasing enemy attacks against DMZ outposts were all we needed to know that NVA presence was increasing, not decreasing.

In the spring of '67, the so called "Hill Fights" were just beginning as the NVA began their push to make Khe Sanh a repeat of the French Dien Bien Phu defeat 13 years earlier. The battle of Dien Bien Phu in 1954 dashed France's hopes of reasserting their pre-World War II colonial holdings in Southeast Asia. But, a half year after I departed Vietnam when the NVA's six month siege of Khe Sanh began in January 1968, the outcome would be different. With the help of concentrated precision air strikes

Heading west toward Khe Sanh our two-ship, HMM-164 flight passed the Rockpile and razorback hills.

from B-52s and other aircraft, a robust marine defense and continuous aerial resupply, the NVA could not sustain the attack and abandoned the effort with heavy but unknown losses in July '68. My small, but personally most dramatic part in the Khe Sanh events, occurred March 16, 1967 on a mission to hill 861 northwest of Khe Sanh when my helicopter was damaged in a mortar attack while extracting wounded marines. The event is described in greater detail later in this book (Khe Sanh Hill 861 Extraction).

H-34 Controlled Flight into Terrain
Accident North of Phu Bai

Four months after joining HMM-164, with a total of 386 hours logged in the CH-46, I was designated a helicopter aircraft commander (HAC) with the first HAC flight on February 2, 1967. An early HAC mission was removing a marine guard who had been killed at a hilltop accident scene northwest of Phu Bai. Everyone on board the CH-34 died in the fiery crash.

As a group, CH-34 helicopter pilots, more so than CH-46 pilots, tended to be averse to instrument flying and would avoid it if they possibly could. This CH-34 crew was picking their way back to Phu Bai in low clouds and low visibility and flew into the hillside. The impact destroyed the helicopter and its mostly magnesium airframe burned like a chemistry lab experiment. When I spiraled down to the small clearing near the hilltop, the accident scene was mostly scorched white from the intense fire with the partially melted remains of the helicopter's R-1820 radial engine and parts of the rotor head all that was distinguishable.

The limp marine we loaded into our CH-46 was part of the security perimeter detail dropped in after the accident and he had been hit by an NVA sniper. We lifted out of the zone and I headed at maximum speed to get the man to a medical facility. The crew chief reported on the interphone that there was no need to fly so fast because the marine was dead. I kept up the speed because I thought the crew chief might be wrong and that there still might be a chance for the poor guy. But the crew chief turned out to be right. So because the CH-34 HAC opted to pick his way back to Phu Bai beneath the low hanging clouds and fog rather than climbing above the clouds and getting a ground controlled radar approach to Phu Bai, he and his crew were lost, his helicopter destroyed, and the young marine sent in to guard the crash site perimeter also died.

A Close One and Nobody Knew Nuth'n

As a newly-minted aircraft commander, I was flying straight and level at 2000 feet on a routine resupply mission about 20 miles south of Da Nang. We were flying over the coastal flatlands with its small thatched villages, rice paddies, and meandering rivers when my crew and I came seconds from becoming a fratricide casualty. By then, VC activity had increased substantially south of Da Nang and air strikes and large scale marine sweeps with supporting artillery fire missions were common in the area. Suddenly, without any radio warning from Landshark, the mission coordinating authority, several large explosions detonated in the rice paddies directly in front of us. The blasts were too large for a grenade or a mortar and obviously came from friendly artillery.

We had earlier checked with Landshark for "Save a Plane" artillery advisories which were transmitted as TACAN distance and bearing coordinates defining firing position, maximum trajectory height and impact point. A typical advisory would be "artillery firing from Da Nang TACAN 180 at 10 miles to Da Nang TACAN 220 at 20 miles, maximum height 15,000 feet."

We used the cockpit radio magnetic indicator compass rose as a plotting board to determine if our projected flight path intersected the artillery trajectory and if so we would change course. Following the explosions, we immediately checked again and the report was negative. We had no way of knowing the source of the firing, but it was unsettling to learn that nobody knew nuth'n and we came close to being just another fratricide statistic.

Night Extraction That Thankfully Wasn't

Flying with a recently arrived copilot, we were fragged for a multi-aircraft night extraction of Hmong scouts and their advisors who were being pursued under fire from an NVA force in the highlands northwest of Phu Bai near Ashau Valley.

Initially the plan was to resupply the group, but their plight was becoming desperate so the decision was made to extract them. Accordingly, I had my crew chief unload the ammo we had planned to deliver to the Hmongs. Several other CH-46s were similarly unloaded at Phu Bai. Then we lifted off and headed northwest into the night toward the jungle highlands. Arriving over the area, about 25 miles northwest of Phu Bai, fixed wing aircraft were dropping parachute flares which drifted down through our orbiting gaggle of helicopters. I couldn't see the landing area and just avoiding the flares and monitoring air-to-air UHF communications and FM ground communications absorbed most of my concentration. My copilot was so new in country that he wasn't much help.

A couple of helicopters managed to descend amid the flares and confusion into the zone and after a short time, it was my turn to head down. I was to be the last helicopter to pluck the remaining trapped group from the clutches of the

NVA. The problem was I couldn't see the landing area to set up the approach. My plan was to rely on the FM radio to get directions from the advisors on the ground. So I lowered the collective and began a shallow descent, rolling out on what I thought was a reasonable final approach heading. The only height reference being our radio altimeters because pressure altimeters only provided height above sea level rather than actual separation from the hills and ridgelines. Then a most pleasant message came up on the FM. It was the HAC who just departed the zone below. He transmitted, "I've got the last of them."

Pulling up at the last moment amid the flares and cacophony of UHF and FM radio chatter was a feeling of relief I will always remember.

Arriving at Phu Bai, the Hmongs and their advisors happily disembarked and we shut down and headed for the relative comfort of the transient hooches. At that point, we learned just how basic the lives of these Hmongs were. For crude as our base was with its "four holer" heads, the Hmongs were accustomed to squatting off trails and in rice paddies, didn't use such facilities, and didn't know quite how to proceed. They adapted by squatting rather than sitting on the hole cut out, aiming as best they could at the opening below.

A Rescue in Laos

January 27, 1967 was a particularly bad day. Two CH-46's from HMM-265 had been shot down at Phou Loutoukou Ridge just inside Laos near the northwest corner of South Vietnam while attempting to extract a recon patrol being chased by NVA's. The first helicopter was hit in the zone and the second on short final approach. A third CH-46 from HMM-164 flown by Major J.D. Watson, a new HAC, crashed late that evening about a mile east of the other two CH-46s, most likely after inadvertently flying into high terrain. A Huey gunship from VMO-2, flying through fog-shrouded hills nearby, also crashed, killing the copilot and injuring the other three crewmembers.

The downed CH-46 helicopter crews and the trapped recons on the ridge were coming under periodic machine gun fire, small arms fire, and infantry assaults. Many were wounded. A total of 31 marines were now surrounded by the NVA. What started out as a dicey recon emergency extraction was turning into a major encounter inside Laos where marines weren't supposed to be. Fixed wing jets made runs on the assaulting NVAs, their bomb impacts hitting so close that NVA body parts showered into the marine's defensive position. Meanwhile, back at the Dong Ha marine base, plans were underway for a multi-helicopter rescue effort for the morning of January 28th.

Chuck Pitman, a solid, level-headed leader, (who later rose to the rank of Lieutenant General), led the six-helicopter rescue mission. Some helicopters carried marine reinforcements and all had cases of ammunition. Major Pitman decided that an extraction was the best option and ordered the extra ammunition be tossed out to accommodate a speedy extraction.

Vince Tesoluv and I were in the last CH-46 and were ordered to recover Major Watson and his downed group across the valley. As the other helicopters headed for the primary recovery LZ, Vince and I circled toward the east, peering down to locate Major Watson's downed helicopter or any sign of his group. Almost immediately, I sighted a red panel spread out on a knoll clearing marking the downed group's position. We made contact on the FM and Vince spiraled down and landed.

Either the NVA were unaware of Major Watson's downed helicopter or they decided that the action across the valley needed to be dealt with first, because the extraction went without a hitch or a shot fired. Duffy Du Friend, a marine lieutenant assigned to Dong Ha's defense unit who volunteered to go along on the mission, was among the first into our helicopter and he bounded up to the cockpit, all smiles. With everyone onboard, Vince lifted out of the clearing and we rejoined the flight, which by then had extracted all the marines across the valley. In a move we all heartily agreed with, Major Pitman ordered the downed helicopters be destroyed, rather than left for future retrieval.

Zero- Zero GCA at Phu Bai

Always at the back of my mind in Vietnam was the need to become the most proficient instrument pilot that I could be for sheer survival and in anticipation of pursuing a career in the airlines. Although the First Marine Air Wing commander waived instrument proficiency checks for in-country pilots to accommodate more pressing flying needs, I also had my priorities and arranged to keep my instrument rating current. And as a HAC, I took every opportunity to fly on instruments on non-combat positioning flights between bases at Marble Mountain, Phu Bai, Dong Ha and Khe Sanh.

Early one February morning, we were assigned a resupply mission from the Phu Bai base. My copilot was Monty Nelson, a competent, sharp-tongued fellow with a quick wit who was known not to suffer quietly the misjudgments or errors of the HACs he was ordered to fly with.

During the monsoon months along the coastal plain, morning fog commonly occurred shortly after sunrise and would persist sometimes for hours until sunlight heated the still air enough to burn it off. And this was just such a morning. A few minutes after taking off, it quickly became apparent the morning fog was fast enveloping the

The Phu Bai airfield and sprawling base complex in the spring of 1967.The runway is at the top in the sandy area.

entire area. And although we could navigate on TACAN to the approximate area of the landing coordinates, ground features were rapidly disappearing beneath the thickening fog layer. There was nothing else to do but abort the mission and return to Phu Bai to await better ground visibility. CH-34s that had launched from Phu Bai around the same time were also aborting their missions and returning to base.

Approaching Phu Bai from the north, I could see the fog had not formed as densely near the airfield so, with an eye to exploiting every opportunity for instrument proficiency training, I requested a few practice radar directed approaches known as GCAs, short for ground controlled approach. During a GCA, the radar controller directs the pilot down a precise glide path to the runway, providing heading and rate of descent instructions to within a hundred feet above the runway with continuing advisories all the way to touchdown.

The GCA controller was happy to oblige because practice for me also meant practice for him and helicopter pilots generally didn't use his services, which he mainly provided to arriving fixed wing transports when the weather was down. And there were no fixed wing arrivals in the vicinity, so we had the controller's undivided attention.

The first GCA approach in light fog was routine and we waved off at the 100 foot decision height with the runway well in view and were directed around for another approach. But on vectors for the second approach, the fog had thickened, completely obscuring the ground from about 200 feet down to the surface. Above this white carpet, the sun shone brightly and visibility was unlimited. The second approach was for real and this time the fog was dense. I flew the approach as precisely as I could, making small heading and sink rate adjustments as the controller instructed. At decision height, 100 feet above the ground, there was only dense fog ahead and I began the missed approach. Climbing through 200 feet, we broke out into the clear.

Monty looked over at me and said, "Okay, this was your idea, now what?" It was a Hobson's choice. Fog had rendered the airport below landing visibility minimums. We had been airborne about 30 minutes already and we could divert to the Marble Mountain base about 40 miles south, but our assignment was to support operations out of Phu Bai. Another alternative was to land on a clear hill top above the fog to the west in the highlands and wait for the fog to burn off. But then, we would have been a sitting duck for any NVA or VC that happened to be about. The only other alternative was to fly the GCA right down to the runway. I chose the latter. The controller vectored us around to the north, then east and finally southwest to intercept the final approach course...all this in the sunny, crystal clear visibility of the Phu Bai morning.

I kept the speed up at 100 knots until we turned final, and then slowed to 80 knots. Passing 500 feet with the white fog layer just below us, we slowed to 60 knots to reduce the glide path sink rate to around 300 feet per minute, which would allow more time to spot the runway.

We entered the fog about 200 feet above the airport with the helicopter's automatic trim system doing a good job holding speed at 60 knots. In the calm morning air, only small corrections of a degree or two were necessary to stay on course and with no turbulence, sink rate control presented no problems. Precision approach radar controllers must keep up a continual stream of instructions lest pilots think a communications breakdown has occurred. In such circumstances pilots must pull up and climb away quickly, a procedure known as a missed approach.

But our controller was rock solid and as we descended, his reassuring voice continued with minor heading and sink rate instructions: "Going slightly right, turn left two degrees," then, "On-course–on-glidepath." Passing 100 feet on the radio altimeter, I could see straight down through the chin bubble and to the round sandy Vietnamese grave plots that bordered the approach end of the runway, but ahead there was just milky white fog. The GCA controller kept talking: "On course, on glidepath." As the radio altimeter needle swept through 50 feet, the dashed white runway centerline markings appeared through the mist and then I could make out the textured runway pavement. I let the helicopter continue descending to touchdown. Horizontal visibility was less than 50 feet and we had no idea where the runway turnoffs were, so we just taxied slowly ahead until a turnoff presented itself, then continued slowly along until we found our way to the ramp.

Meanwhile several returning H-34s were still in the air and those crews faced the same dilemma: how to get down before running out of fuel. But as a group, "Thirty-four drivers" were more inclined to visual contact flying and they had no stomach for a solid instrument GCA approach down to the ground. Instead, when they flew over the field, they found that although horizontal visibility was near zero in the fog, they could just barely see the ground if they looked straight down. So their solution was to overhead the field using the TACAN and look straight down to spot the runway in the heavy mist. Then they slowed to around 40 knots, lowered the collective pitch and auto rotated down through the soup, flaring at the last moment and rolling onto the pavement. It was crude but it worked...but just barely. Forty-five minutes later, sunshine burned off the fog and blue skies returned.

Recovering the (Ryan Firebee) Reconnaissance Drone from the South China Sea

One afternoon, I was assigned to recover a turbo jet Ryan Firebee reconnaissance drone from the South China Sea. The drone had flown over North Vietnam gathering intelligence, and then to Da Nang where its engine shut down, a parachute deployed and it floated down to the sea near Monkey Mountain. After splashing down, Navy divers dropped from a helicopter, attached floatation devices and a drag chute and deployed dye marker to make the drone easier to spot in the sea.

Our job was straightforward enough, according to the mission briefer: to hover about 10 feet directly above the drone while the diver engaged a vertical reach pendant suspended from the helicopter's cargo hook. Then we were to pluck the drone straight up into a high hover to allow water to drain from its openings. After that, simply fly it back to Da Nang at low speed.

During an earlier recovery mission that day, the crew chief reported the pilot had difficulty positioning the helicopter over the drone. The mission devolved into lots of left, right, forward and back commands as the crew chief, looking down through the belly hatch, directed the aircraft commander for the hook-up, while divers in the water struggled amid rotor downwash and ocean spray. With that sobering report in mind, we lifted off Marble Mountain Air Facility and headed north over Da Nang Bay, then out into the South China Sea. By then, Marine CH-34's had dropped Navy divers near the drone. They circled about a mile away, waiting to recover the divers after I recovered the drone. The Firebee was easy to spot in the middle of a large splotch of aqua green dye marker. I swung the CH-46 into the wind about a quarter mile from the drone and descended, slowing to a high hover above the dye marker, then, guessing I was about over the drone, descended close to the waves for the hook-up. Within a few seconds the crew chief reported the diver had attached the pendant to the drone. Plucking the drone from the sea took more power than I anticipated but it popped free and the engine torque required to hover dropped off as sea water drained from the Firebee's openings.

The whole operation took just a few minutes and when we radioed the Air Force coordinator that we were headed toward the Da Nang airport to drop it off, he expressed surprise that it had all happened so fast. At Da Nang Air Base, the Air Force ground crew directed us to a spot on the ramp where I gently lowered the drone to the concrete, pickled off the pendant and then landed to retrieve it. Soon we were on our way back to Marble Mountain. It was the only at-sea pick up I ever made.

Cubi Point Jungle Survival School
and the Officers' Club

About midway through the WESTPAC tour and looking for a way out of Vietnam for a while, I requested and was granted orders to a three-day jungle survival training course at NAS Cubi Point on Subic Bay in the Philippines. The last night of the course was to be spent in the nearby jungle putting to use survival techniques we learned the previous two days; things like extracting drinkable liquid from vines and cooking insects, lizards and other small jungle creatures in bamboo shoots. The training orders included several extra days in the Philippines, so it was a kind of an informal R & R trip which didn't count as an R&R of which we were granted two during the combat tour. I made the most of those extra days by arranging for my fiancée to fly from the West Coast to meet me in Manila after the training.

Philippine locals who knew their way around the jungle ran the classes. To earn extra money, they fashioned makeshift machetes from automobile leaf springs and sold them to course attendees as jungle survival tools. They were crude but functional and came in handy in the jungle. Everyone bought one.

The short trek into the jungle was a harbinger of the uncomfortable night to come. Students separated into pairs and we set about pitching camp and scavenging about for edible berries, fruits and creatures to capture and cook in the bamboo shoots we fashioned into cooking receptacles. As the sun sank and the jungle grew dark except for our small camp fire, we gradually became aware of how uncomfortable the next 10 or so hours were going to be.

Leo Farrell, a fellow officer from the squadron, and I shared a camp fire and had about the same level of discomfort with our surroundings. We agreed that a night in the jungle wasn't necessary to reinforce the techniques of drinking from vines and cooking the jungle's small inhabitants in bamboo shoots. So we decided to leave quietly. Our encampment was only about a 15-minute hike beyond the base's roads and buildings. We began walking through the jungle, backtracking on what we thought was the approximate path. But in the dark, we lost our way and hearing distant laughter and following the glow of electric lights, we emerged at an enlisted housing area swimming pool. It was still early evening and the place was filled with kids splashing about and their moms and pool staff looking on. We must have been a sight emerging from the jungle in our dirty utility uniforms, flashlights in hand. We asked if there was a public phone and it was pointed out to us. I called a cab and, in short order, we were whisked to the BOQ. A quick shower and a change into civilian clothes transitioned Leo and me for a more comfortable evening. We split up, agreeing to meet in the BOQ lobby about 0400 for the trip back to the jungle. My destination was the Cubi Point Officers' Club.

The club was a raucous place that night. An attack carrier had arrived recently and the pilots were an understandably exuberant lot, glad to be off their ship where they flew strikes into North Vietnam. It was a carefree time, and they were making the most of the night. I seated myself at a table off in a corner and, watching the animated scene at the bar, began comparing their life with ours in Vietnam. These fighter and attack pilots saw the war from a different perspective. They made high speed stabs into North Vietnam, dropped bombs, then dashed back to their carrier. Of course, like us, some didn't make it back. But they slept in clean bunks, ate meals on tablecloths served by stewards in the officers wardroom, and saw movies at night in their ready room. Not bad! Our life was the opposite: we flew low and slow, alighting on hilltops, splashing down in rice paddies, or hovering above the jungle. We slept on cots in hooches with sand-bagged bunkers outside. Speed was an attack and fighter pilot's friend and they had lots of it. Our maximum speed would barely budge their airspeed pointers off the peg. And if I told them that I sometimes spiraled into a landing zone with an extra 20 knots of airspeed to make us harder to hit, they'd just chuckle and wonder silently how such a sliver of velocity could make any difference at all. It probably didn't and, in fact, those extra knots made it harder to stop in the landing zone and sometimes caused overrun accidents. And the smart Viet Cong and NVA gunners knew that no matter what we did on the approach, we soon must hover or land... and they just waited. Then the waiter arrived and returned my wandering mind to the matter at hand. I ordered a beer and lobster.

To me, that night at the Cubi Point Officers' Club was nirvana. At another time and place, it would have been just another good lobster dinner. But after six months of in-country chow hall fare and C rations, it was a tasty, delightful, luxurious, and memorable dinner. And after the meal back at the BOQ, I got five hours of sleep on a real mattress. Delightful!

My alarm went off at 0400 and it was time to put the utilities back on, lace up my boots and head for the BOQ lobby to meet Leo for the cab ride back to the edge of the jungle. Dawn was breaking as we reached the rest of our survival classmates who were just rising after the misery of their night. Leo and I said nothing, just gathered our gear, and hiked out with the rest of the class.

Temperamentally, Leo and I had little in common, he being a more rambunctious, extroverted fellow. Since we were both HACs and didn't hang out at the club over beers, our only connection was the joint missions we occasionally flew. But I'll always be grateful to Leo for a mission he took in my place on March 13, 1967 at Dong Ha, solely by the luck of the draw. A wounded marine needed to be hoisted out of a contentious zone near the DMZ. A CH-34 crew had already been shot up in their unsuccessful attempt and the mission was assigned to a CH-46 crew, but the aircraft needed a 150 hoist cable to reach through tall tree cover. Leo and I ordered our crew chiefs to check the length of our hoists since earlier manufactured CH-46A's had only 100-foot hoist cables. Leo's had the 150 cable and mine didn't. He took the mission and was shot down, and he and his crew spent the night with the grunts out in the field.

Aborted Medevac Mission to the Repose

As the war escalated in the spring of 1967, casualties in the northern I Corps mounted and two hospital ships, the *Repose* and the *Sanctuary*, were stationed off the coast to receive them.

Huey Walsh and I were HACs in a two aircraft section assigned to Phu Bai and one night, we were fragged to transport two helicopter loads of stretchered and sedated marine medevacs out to the *USS Repose* about 15 miles off the coast. Corpsmen, assisted by our crew chief and gunner, configured the helicopter's interior for the stretchers which were suspended bunk-like one atop the other in layers of three. Then the medevacs were brought on board, their stretchers fastened into the suspended mounts. We had about 12 or so stretchered marines on board with several corpsmen attending the wounded marines, many of whom had IV bottles attached and hanging above them. By the time we launched, night had settled in and the helicopter's cabin was illuminated with dim red lights to preserve night vision.

We lifted off and headed east over the coastline and into the pitch blackness of the South China Sea. Ahead and out of sight was the *USS Repose*, a 520 foot World War II era hospital ship with a helicopter landing pad on its stern. The landing pad, more suitable for the smaller H-34, was just barely large enough to accommodate our much longer tandem rotor CH-46, but just barely. Forward of the landing pad loomed the ship's superstructure and smoke stack. Approaches and departures were made at a 45-degree angle to the ship's centerline, and a large X painted diagonally on the landing pad provided pilots with the proper lineup as they angled in from the port or starboard side, depending on the wind. When properly positioned on the deck, the CH-46's fuselage is 45-degrees to the ship's centerline, and the cockpit is near the deck's edge with the view ahead mostly ocean, or in this case, blackness. At night, the deck's edge lights provided a three-dimensional reference for a safe approach and landing.

U.S. Navy Photo

The hospital Ship USS Repose stationed in the South China Sea off northern Quang Tri Provence in the spring of 1967 received numerous casualties from the fighting along the DMZ.

Huey made radio contact with the ship and the ship provided a DF steer pointing the way to her. Looking back into the cabin's dim red lights I could see the corpsmen moving among the stretchers, tending the wounded. In a few minutes we would accomplish the landing checklist, setting the main gear brakes and locking the nose wheel to prevent movement on the small deck once the helicopter touched down.

Then the ship's radioman transmitted some troubling information. The ship had lost a portion of its electrical power which, in turn, extinguished the landing pad's edge lights. Deck border lights are critical because they provide height and closure rate perspective at night when there are no other visual references for the approach. Lacking deck lights, the only deck spotting illumination would come from our nose-mounted controllable landing spot light, its beam directed by a small coolie hat switch on the collective pitch lever. Using thumb movements, a pilot can control the beam by toggling the switch forward or backward, left or right.

Faced with the prospect of a night landing on the Repose's stern with only our helicopter's searchlight concerned me. Having landed several times on the Repose during daylight, I knew just a few feet separated the forward rotor disk from the ship's superstructure and there was little margin for error. And misjudging the closure rate and overshooting or otherwise striking the ship could have resulted in an uncontrolled ditching and the almost certain drowning of all those in the back.

My assessment was that a landing under those conditions wasn't worth the risk and I waved off and circled. Huey, on the other hand, said he'd give it a try and he landed successfully and offloaded his casualties. My hat's off to him for his nerve and airmanship. We flew back to Phu Bai and offloaded the medevacs. I had no idea how badly wounded they were and I hoped that delaying their flight to the Repose until morning didn't exacerbate their condition or result in anyone's preventable death.

Khe Sanh Hill 861 Medevac

Early in 1967, NVA troops began moving in around the Khe Sanh Combat Base and fierce skirmishes on the hills northwest of the base became more frequent. What followed in the next few months became known as the "Hill Fights," which continued through May 1967 and later evolved to the siege of Khe Sanh lasting into April 1968.

Russ Verbael and I were HACs in a two aircraft section supporting marines northwest of Khe Sanh on hills 861, 881 north and 881 south. The military identifies hills that are not otherwise named by their height in meters above sea level, hill 861 being 2825 feet. That afternoon our mission was

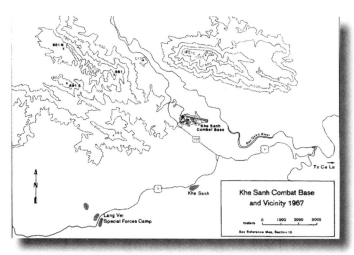

The U.S. Marines in Vietnam, Fighting the North Vietnamese 1967
Headquarters, USMC, Washington, D.C

to medevac casualties off 861. We departed Khe Sanh in a loose, two aircraft tactical left echelon and I stayed high as Russ landed, retrieved the medevacs and returned to Khe Sanh. Shortly thereafter, another medevac order came in, but Russ's CH-46 developed a mechanical problem, so I took the mission as a single aircraft.

Hill 861 had been largely denuded by mortar blasts and small arms fire and there was no level place to set the helicopter down on the steeply sloping hilltop. The only way in was to hover above the slope, swing the tail around facing the hillside, then back in and lower the aft ramp. Marines on the hilltop remained in their foxholes, largely out of sight. The hovering and backing maneuver took about 10 or 15 seconds. Just as I had the main gear firmly butted against the hillside with the front of the helicopter level out in thin air, my co-pilot, Bob Godwin, announced over the ICS that we were taking mortar fire on his side. I couldn't hear the rounds exploding, and initially, I thought since they weren't audible on my side, they were far enough away that we could get the medevacs in and depart before the NVA could adjust their fire. But I could see that Bob was getting frantic and I decided that the best thing to do was return to Khe Sanh. I lifted off, eased the cyclic forward and dove steeply, following the hillside into the valley and back toward Khe Sanh.

On the way in, I reported that we had taken mortar fire and were returning. But no sooner had we landed than the marines on the hilltop were again calling for medevac support because they were taking even more casualties. But as I saw it, the landing area was untenable because the NVA had the hilltop zeroed in and the steep terrain and small unobstructed area on the hilltop prevented us from quickly swooping in and scooping up the wounded before the NVA could bring their mortar fire down on us.

We discussed the predicament on the FM grunt frequency. A Marine Huey gunship pilot broke into the discussion and reported that he thought he had the NVA mortar position sighted and if we came up low from the south and arced around the hillside to the landing point, he would make a simultaneous run on the mortar position, allowing us to swoop in and get the medevacs. I was incredulous about the sighting because the dense tree canopies on the surrounding hills were an opaque, green tapestry, masking everything underneath. But the mission was urgent and even though the gunship pilot's premise was shaky, I felt it was worth the effort. I transmitted back: "It's against my better judgment, but we'll give it a try."

Considering the hilltop's approximate 2800 foot elevation and the warm temperature on that March afternoon, I determined we could safely remove seven wounded and transmitted that information to the entrenched grunts on FM. Any more than that wouldn't allow us to lift off and hover out of ground effect, and we would settle uncontrollably into the sloping hillside and crash. Bob didn't say anything and the crew chief and gunner were quiet as well. We knew it was a very dicey situation.

So off we went, flying low and climbing with the rising terrain toward the south slope of hill 861. Arriving near the top, I slowed and flew around the crest to the blast-denuded hillside clearing. Swinging the helicopter's nose off to the left and backing into the hillside took a few seconds longer than the first effort, but we succeeded in butting the main gear wheels against the hillside and the crew chief lowered the ramp. The marines on the hilltop broke from their cover and began assisting the wounded aboard. Meanwhile, the Huey gunship pilot made his run, firing rockets and machine guns toward what he thought was the mortar position. But the NVA weren't where he was shooting, or if they were, they weren't phased by what was coming at them. I suspect the former.

As I look back on the event, the NVA, seeing that we were maneuvering to land, began firing 82MM mortar rounds. There was no need for bracketing rounds; the hilltop was already zeroed in. And while I was backing into the hillside, the rounds were likely on their way skyward and soon would arc down on top of us.

The helicopter was butted against the hillside less than half a minute, and by then, seven medevac casualties and seven or eight grunts helping them (I never knew the exact number) were onboard when the first mortar round hit close by on the right side. Instinctively, I pulled in collective pitch and lifted off the hillside, then put in forward cyclic, pitching the nose into a dive. But the helicopter was grossly overloaded, probably by about 1200 to 1500 pounds. Rotor RPM decayed quickly to 88 percent. I dared not increase collective pitch anymore because below that RPM, generators drop off the line, the stabilization system drops out, lift decreases, and control gets mushy. Holding rotor 88 percent RPM, we had to accept a sink rate that barely kept the helicopter above the hillside's tree tops. Fortunately, after a few hundred feet of descent, the hill sloped away more steeply, and then sharply dropped away into the valley. I eased the cyclic forward and decreased collective pitch, regaining airspeed and 100 percent rotor RPM and dove off into the Valley, turning southeast toward Khe Sanh. There were no caution lights and the helicopter seemed to respond to control inputs, except for a shuddering vibration.

The whole event from the mortar's impact to the point when it was apparent we had safely cleared the terrain and regained safe rotor RPM took perhaps no more than 20 seconds. It was a period of intense focus, limiting collective pitch to keep rotor RPM at 88 percent, as we settled down the hillside while steering the helicopter toward the valley below. We radioed ahead that we were coming in with the medevacs and that the helicopter had been mortared. At Khe Sanh, corpsmen and marines were on hand to remove the wounded troops.

Before I shut down, Russ ran up to the helicopter and speaking into the external hand phone, excitedly suggested that we could continue the mission by landing on the defilade side of Hill 861, out of the direct sight of NVA mortar crews. But I would have none of it. I had been mortared twice attempting to get the wounded out, the second time nearly losing the helicopter and everyone inside. Besides that, our helicopter was damaged in the attack, possibly to the point of being unairworthy. There comes a time when discretion trumps valor — when valor does more harm than good. I responded that I wasn't about to go up there and try it again, but if he wanted to, he could take my helicopter and do it. We then cut the engine condition levers and shut down. By the time the rotors stopped and we finished the shut-down, only one wounded marine, swathed in an arm bandage remained. He said, "Thank you, sir. " I smiled and said: "You're welcome."

A look around the helicopter revealed that the mortar round had probably passed through the rotor disc and detonated below the fuselage on the sloping hillside. The blast had gone nearly straight up, peppering the belly with about 150 holes with some shrapnel damage to the aft rotors. There was also some minor deformation near the blade tips, most likely caused from striking small trees while backing into the hillside.

While my damage assessment was going on, Russ's crew chief had done repairs and gotten his helicopter flyable. They quickly loaded on marine reinforcements and ammunition, fired up, and took off toward hill 861. I watched as Russ's helicopter climbed northwest toward the embattled hilltop. A marine communications jeep parked out near the runway with a gaggle of grunts around it monitored the action via the jeep's FM radio. With nothing else to do, I left the aircraft and headed toward the jeep. By then, Russ's CH-46, maneuvering low around the hills toward Hill 861, had disappeared from view.

When I reached the jeep, the marine radio operator looked up and calmly said, "They just crashed." My feeling at that moment was of being completely spent. There was nothing I could do and in Russ's zeal to help the embattled grunts, he apparently overshot the zone and crashed. Russ later speculated that he may have taken fire as he approached the touchdown point but that couldn't be confirmed. Years later, after reading an account of that day, I learned that two corpsmen had been killed in the mortar barrage which had nearly destroyed our helicopter. (U.S. Marines in Vietnam, Fighting the North Vietnamese, 1967, History and Museums Division, Headquarters, USMC, Washington, D.C.)

Night Carrier Qualification
on the USS Princeton (LPH 5)

In late March 1967 with two months to go in-country before rotating back to the U.S., we relatively short time pilots were given the option of remaining with HMM-164, which was to deploy with the Special Landing Force aboard the carrier USS Princeton LPH-5, or be transferred to another squadron based in-country. With the war becoming more intense by the month and the chance to live on board ship, we all thought the choice was a no-brainer. On top of that, I learned the ship was scheduled to spend about a month in exercises around Okinawa and the Philippines. That made the choice even more appealing. The only catch was that to assure unit cohesiveness, we would be required to extend our WESTPAC tour an additional month. So instead of rotating back in May, we would return sometime in June. Still, it was an easy decision and we all went for it.

My log book shows the squadron flew aboard the Princeton on 3 April '67. Heading north along the coast, we brought on board a battalion of marines rotating out of country back to Okinawa. Life aboard ship was a pleasant change from the hooches of Marble Mountain, Phu Bai, Dong Ha and Khe Sanh. On the Princeton, we slept in bunk beds on clean sheets, no more hooch cot. Stewards served meals in the officers wardroom and there were nightly movies in the ready room. At night, as we steamed northeast to Okinawa, I'd sometimes walk on the flight deck under a canopy of stars enveloped in the warm wind of the South China Sea. It was another world out at sea and on the whole, quite enjoyable.

We had barely settled in to our quarters when word came down that all pilots would be night carrier qualified as soon as possible. It didn't sit well with the junior officers who wanted more time before flying the low, 400 foot carrier pattern in the darkness of the ocean. But orders were orders and it made sense to be night mission ready aboard ship. So, four days after coming aboard, aircraft commanders paired up and about an hour after sunset, several helicopters launched into the blackness, entered a race track pattern at 400 feet and 80 knots on the Princeton's port side and commenced night carrier qualifications.

Paul Albano, another squadron captain and HAC, and I took turns in the right seat where the HAC flies in a helicopter. As a precaution, I set the radio altimeter height bug to 100 feet. It would illuminate an amber light on the altimeter if we inadvertently descended at an inappropriate point in the traffic pattern. My log book shows that I made seven landings that night. Then Paul did the same. After we completed the required night landings, signalmen with lighted wands directed us to our deck spot, the nose gear and main gear were chained to the deck and we shut down, grateful that night qualifications were behind us. It was intense flying and mostly on instruments.

CH-46As of HMM-164 spotted on the flight deck of LPH 5, USS Princeton, in the South China Sea, March 1967.

The following day our senior officers, all majors who headed up operations, maintenance and material, and administration, would try their hand at night carrier qualification. In general, the squadron's senior lieutenants and captains tended to be sharper aviators simply because after nearly a year in country they did a lot more flying than the more deskbound senior officers. By then, those of us who transferred to the squadron from HMM-265 were captains and tended to be a crusty lot, confident and for the most part, capable in our flying. A subtle divide existed between the junior officers (lieutenants and captains) and the squadron's senior officers, all majors, and the skipper, a lieutenant colonel known as the "old man," an amiable fellow in his mid-forties. Part of it had to do with perceptions of flying skills. Junior officers, in general, thought themselves more agile and capable fliers than the senior officers, who for the most part, although there were exceptions, were perceived as a plodding group better suited to desk functions. Tomorrow, we'd watch the majors from "vulture's row," the open deck on the Princeton's superstructure just behind the bridge, to see if perception and practice merged. And it would be quite a show.

The next day passed uneventfully as the Princeton steamed north on tranquil seas toward Okinawa. When night fell, we assembled in the wardroom for dinner, filled with anticipation of the night's activities. After dinner, we headed for the ready room, taking seats in the rear as the majors briefed their carrier qualification period. By the time they finished, twilight had faded and they emerged onto the flight deck into a black, moonless night. From vultures row, about a half dozen of us stared down on the flight deck as APUs started and the helicopter's red rotating beacons swept red flashes across the carrier's island superstructure. Then the CH-46's twin engines fired up, rotors were engaged and the sound of turbines and rotors overwhelmed all other sounds.

One by one, the three CH-46s lifted into a hover and then slid diagonally off the port side, gaining airspeed and climbing out ahead of the ship into a night as black as coal. We watched as their red rotating beacons turned downwind and headed back toward the ship. The first helicopter to turn base leg got low, nearly descending into the sea. It pulled up and turned sharply to the "fox corpen" (the Navy's term for the ship's aircraft recovery course), climbing away for another try. The next helicopter turned base leg but was way too fast and high. It whizzed over the flight deck behind the island, waving off up the Princeton's starboard side! We anticipated a memorable show, but this exceeded our expectations. The third helicopter, after a shaky approach, successfully landed. On the next pass all the helicopters made it back to the flight deck but to everyone's surprise, they didn't lift off. Instead, we watched in astonishment as they all shut down after a total of four landings between the three aircraft! The majors had been so spooked by their carnival of aeronautical ineptitude that good judgment overcame pride and they called it quits for the night.

We quickly left our perch on vulture's row and raced to the ready room to watch the majors file in for their curtain call. Bounding down several decks, we made it before they arrived and took seats in the back, striking nonchalant poses as though we had been there all evening. They filed in, harried, unsnapping their Mae Wests and flopping into seats, mumbling about how black the night was and how hairy their flying was. We sat silently in the back. They would try again the next day, only earlier after sunset and before the horizon completely disappeared into pitch blackness. We junior officers never mentioned that night, but a pecking order of relative competence had been established and there was no doubt where the majors stood in the group.

In fairness to the majors, the Navy's helicopter night landing pattern was poorly thought out. Unlike fixed wing patterns where aircraft fly level until turning onto the final approach course and then are guided down a precise visual descent path all the way to touchdown, helicopter pilots had no such glideslope references coming aboard the Princeton. It was entirely instrument flying with just a glance at the ship out the cockpit's left window before turning base leg abeam the ship's bow. The descending, decelerating turn is continued, largely by reference to cockpit instruments until abeam the flight deck at a speed matching the ship's forward speed, generally about 25 knots indicated airspeed. The aircraft commander then must spot the LSE's (landing signal enlisted) bulb-lighted uniform and lighted wands which direct him to slide the helicopter diagonally over the flight deck to the landing spot. Complicating this complex and demanding maneuver was the need to maintain at least 40 knots indicated airspeed (the engine failure wave off speed) until fairly close to the ship. In summary, it was unnecessarily demanding flying when clearly there was a better, safer way. After initial night carrier qualification, pilots never flew the standard NATOPS night carrier pattern, choosing instead to approach from astern or abeam with the ship in sight at all times. In low visibility, night or day, radar controllers directed pilots to the ship from astern in a manner similar to fixed wing carrier approaches.

A Change of Plans

Arriving off the coast of Okinawa, the squadron flew the embarked marines ashore and for the next several days, we just made occasional administrative flights to shore bases as the ship cruised leisurely off the coast. On the fourth day, I awoke to a subtle tremor in the ship. The 888-foot Princeton was cutting a fast path through the sea and anyone on board who was even even slightly attuned to the ship's rythms could sense it. Something had changed and the ship was moving more purposefully somewhere.

At breakfast in the officer's wardroom, we learned that the Princeton's previous itinerary was cancelled and we were headed back to Vietnam. We would immediately fly a fresh battalion of marines aboard from Okinawa as we steamed south. Along the way, we would join other ships in the special landing force for a helicopter coastal assault north of Hue and later, for the first time in the war, an assault into the DMZ. To us old salts from HMM-265 who had extended our tours for what was advertised as an at-sea R&R, our expectations were dashed. Once again, we'd be off the 17th parallel, putting the newly embarked battalion into the thick of it. From Khe Sanh in the west and all along the DMZ, the war was heating up and HMM-164 was pressed into service to support it.

CH-46A delivering a 105MM artillery piece to Con Thien, a marine outpost about six miles northwest of Dong Ha and just south of the DMZ in the spring of 1967. Concurrent with the NVA buildup around Khe Sanh, attacks and artillery barrages east along the DMZ also intensified.

Taking KIAs Back to the Princeton

From April '67 on, we spent almost as much time deployed ashore as on board the Princeton, with frequent shuttle flights from the Khe Sanh, Dong Ha and Phu Bai bases to the ship and supporting SLF vessels. On a refueling stop at the Marine Phu Bai base, we were tasked to return several recently killed marine infantrymen to the Princeton to be refrigerated until they could be transported to Da Nang Air Base's mortuary for shipment to the U.S. The marine helicopter apron at Phu Bai was a short distance from the civil terminal where Air Vietnam, World War II vintage twin engine C-46 Curtis Commando transports routinely came and went with their local passengers. The old concrete terminal building dated back to French Colonial days and had an observation deck on the second level. I watched two red-robed Buddhist monks staring down at our helicopter as the dead marines, still in their blood stained utilities, were carried on board through the aft ramp and laid on the cabin floor. I could only guess what the monks were thinking. But watching them watching us struck me as an incongruous juxtaposition. Like the demoralized ARVN troops, they stared passively as the marines, who had come halfway around the world to fight their battles, were now on their way back home. I also thought about the marine families, who, at that moment, didn't know their sons were gone, and that in their minds, at least for a little while longer, were still alive. With all the dead now stacked on the cabin floor, the crew chief raised the aft ramp. We taxied out to the runway, lifted off, and headed east, climbing over the small coastal villages and rice paddies toward the Princeton, just over the horizon in the South China Sea.

The Night P.T. Looney Died

Captain P.T. Looney was a cheerful, competent aviator, well-liked and a pilot others could count on. May 10, 1967, was the night he died, and his copilot, gunner, and crew chief were wounded trying to extract a marine recon team on Hill 665 north of Khe Sanh. Pilots who weren't flying got a good night's sleep aboard the U.S.S. Princeton. Like so much in life, good and bad fortune hinges simply on time and place, except in war, the chance of bad fortune is magnified by opposing forces. As the "hill fights" continued northwest of Khe Sanh, helicopters from our embarked squadron were commonly assigned four-day detachments ashore to support those operations. On this day, P.T. took the Khe Sanh mission as flight leader of a two aircraft section. The outcome probably wouldn't have been much different for any other pilot. The calculus of war simply caught up with P.T. that night.

With two marines killed and others wounded in the seven-man patrol, the surrounded marines were in a bad way. According to accounts in Marion Starkey's book, *Bonnie-Sue*, and ready room talk aboard ship following the event, the NVA were a savvy lot. They didn't start shooting at P.T's helicopter as it lined up to land, but instead waited until it slowed to a near hover. Then they opened up with everything they had. The helicopter took 48 hits, striking everyone in the crew. P.T. was hit just above his armored chest plate. The bullet deflected off his collar bone and down into his chest, severing arteries and causing massive internal bleeding. The copilot waved off and headed back to Khe Sanh while P.T. crawled out of his seat and lay in the cabin. Marines met the helicopter at Khe Sanh and brought P.T. to the base aid station. I recall from ready room talk that he waved to marines as they carried him off. Doctors couldn't save him and he died a short time later.

P.T.'s cabin on the Princeton was across a passageway from the cabin I shared with a few other captains below the flight deck near the bow. In the next few days, his personal effects were gathered atop his bunk, boxed, and sent to his family. So what did I think of all this? I, and as far as I could tell, the other pilots who had been there for some time, simply took the news in stride and stayed focused on the future, which mainly meant getting out alive. By then, the squadron was about evenly divided between the "old salts" like me, many of whom had transferred into the squadron about eight months earlier from HMM-265 and had been in country for almost a year, and newer lieutenants and majors still getting the hang of things. Many of us had come to Vietnam as lieutenants and copilots but were now aircraft commanders and captains. We knew the country, knew the enemy, knew our aircraft, and for the most part, flew "savvy." That is, we flew conservatively, didn't spiral into zones too fast or too slow, were careful specifying the loads we could carry so we had enough extra power to hover with some safety margin, and in general, avoided dicey situations whenever we could. In short, we minimized the controllable variables that had brought others to grief, all the while knowing that, like P.T., there might come a time when no matter what we did, it would end badly. With orders out of Vietnam just weeks away, we were what marines called "short," and our flying reflected it.

So what happened to those surrounded marines on Hill 665 where P.T. met his end? They hung tight that night. The next morning fixed wing air strikes drove off the North Vietnamese with an unknown number of casualties, and the wounded marines were extracted by a marine Huey helicopter that swooped in and snatched them out.

Instrument Check

Even though instrument checks were waived for in-country marine fliers, I had my own career priorities looking forward to an airline job and wanted to keep my checks current. In retrospect, it didn't make any difference, but that was my mindset at the time.

The operations officer agreed to conduct the check if a suitable mission could be combined with the check flight. The suitable mission came on May 10, 1967 to fly dead marines to Da Nang. They had been killed in action, flown out to the ship and stored in the ship's refrigerators, awaiting transport for embalming and shipment back to the United States.

After a pleasant wardroom breakfast, we adjourned to the ready room and briefed the mission, basically a straight line flight from about 15 miles east of the DMZ in the South China Sea to Da Nang. We picked up our flight gear and weapons and headed up ladders into the carrier's superstructure island and out onto the flight deck. Since the weather was good, I would be under an instrument hood for the entire flight from just after clearing the flight deck to 100 feet above the runway at Da Nang. The hood blocked outside vision, simulating instrument conditions similar to flying in a cloud.

As we completed pre-start procedures, a team of marines brought the sagging green body bags to our helicopter and deposited them on the cabin floor. The ship's refrigeration hadn't done much to prevent decomposition and the rotting smell of the dead filled the helicopter. We opened the cockpit's sliding windows but it didn't do much good, and I felt for the crew chief and gunner back in the cabin who had to breathe in the worst of it.

The flight to Da Nang, mostly off the coast, was uneventful. The smell was with us the whole way no matter how we adjusted the cabin ventilation. Round trip, 2.1 hours, 1.8 hours instrument time under the hood, which included a radar precision approach at Da Nang and a TACAN non-precision approach returning to the ship. After preparation at the Da Nang military mortuary, the marines would be placed in metal caskets, flown back to the United States and given a military funeral. Mission accomplished, instrument check, "complete and satisfactory."

A Mission That Never Came to Pass

As North Vietnamese forces built up in the northern I Corps in the early months of 1967, the United States decided to use Marine Corps helicopters in operations inside Laos. Up until this time, such missions were the province of Air America with an occasional Marine Corps foray near the border.

But when the USS Princeton departed the area for Okinawa in late May, a small contingent of squadron aircraft and crews were assigned back to Marble Mountain. Pilots drew lots, but some were ordered to remain behind. I was among the HACs who returned to Marble Mountain. Shortly after arriving, word went out that Marine markings would be sprayed over in anticipation of using Marine Corps crews and aircraft in Laos. That order, to obliterate U.S. markings, struck me as beyond the pale. After all, who were we fooling? If an unmarked Marine helicopter went down in Laos, who could it possibly belong to other than the U.S.? I resolved to do what I could to avoid being on such a mission. But no Laos flights were assigned and our remaining days were spent flying routine missions uneventfully. In the first week of June, I boarded a C-130 bound for MCAS Futenma on our way back to the U.S. with other held-over squadron pilots.

Coming Home

The MCAS Futenma Officers' Club in Okinawa was a drab place. The most memorable thing about it was a painting of a voluptuous nude lady hanging on the wall behind the bar and a juke box in the corner.

I can't recall if it took nickels or dimes but I distinctly remember repeatedly playing the Animals song, "We Gotta to Get Out of this Place." There was nothing else to think about but the flight back to the West Coast. It was a chartered Northwest 707, non-stop to Travis Air Force Base in northern California. From there, we were bussed to San Francisco International Airport, then a short flight to Los Angeles where my fiancée met me walking off the jetway. A week later we were married.

With a year of active duty remaining, I was ordered to MCAS New River and assigned to HMM-161 to train CH-46 pilots who would soon deploy to Vietnam. The students were a mixed bag; some were "nuggets" straight out of the Naval Air Training Command, the rest were a cadre of salty majors, pried kicking and screaming from Marine jet fighter and attack squadrons. The young lieutenants were an easy-to-train, malleable group. The jet jock majors with their flashy, flight jacket F-4 and A-4 jet squadron patches and lightning bolt adorned helmets were all over the place when it came to competence and their attitude toward training. They went through the same ego-shattering learning curve that we did back in the training command transitioning from fixed wing T-28s to rotorcraft. But switching from a Mach 2+ Phantom jet to an ungainly CH-46, whose 140 knot maximum speed would barely keep a Phantom in the air, was a real come down. Complicating their transition, the tandem rotor CH-46 was a handful to fly, even for an experienced pilot, with the stabilization switched off or disabled. This further frustrated and infuriated many of these high ego senior aviators. How well they fared in training and combat depended largely on their attitude, some succeeded well, while others had a much harder time according to anecdotal reports coming back from WESTPAC.

By then, Boeing was making CH-46D models with more powerful T-58-GE-10 engines rated at 1400 horse power and a maximum takeoff gross weight increase from the CH-46A model's 21,400 pounds to 23,000 pounds, and a five knot higher maximum sea level speed of 145 knots. The spanking new D-models were a joy to climb into, compared to the CH-46As we flew in country. Even though the CH-46A's were only about two years old, helicopters aged fast in Vietnam. They were beat up by hard landings, heavy ammo boxes hauled in and out, leaking sacks of rice, mini jeeps skidding against the cabin's interior, and the constant flow of grunts with their weapons and dirt, plus the ubiquitous fine sand of Vietnam's coastal plain that got into everything. In-country CH-46's were a haggard lot and it's amazing they held up as well as they did.

What didn't change with the D models was the

helicopter's fearful accident record. Concern about CH-46's safety reached the halls of Congress which sent investigators to MCAS New River to interview CH-46 aircraft commanders and others involved with the helicopter's operation. In spite of its record, I had mixed but generally positive feelings toward the aircraft and I passed those views along to the investigators. I felt that way perhaps because pilots develop a relationship with aircraft, especially if they've been through tough times together.

I related to investigators how the CH-46 had stayed together through a mountain top rollover without bursting into flames, and another time had taken small arms hits which disabled systems and still got us safely down. Then there was the mountaintop mortar detonation beneath the helicopter on Hill 861 near Khe Sanh which still allowed me to fly off grossly overloaded with medical evacuees. I went on to tell them that the helicopter had its mechanical issues, but nevertheless was a capable aircraft and I would be confident flying it. The investigators left and we never heard any more about the investigation. But the accidents which were largely related to maintenance and crew errors, continued. After I left the Marine Corps, structural modifications and design enhancements made it a more reliable and capable aircraft and it went on to serve in the Corps for over 48 years.

On July 25, 1968, my last CH-46 flight was logged and my Marine Corps flying days were over. A month later, I would join Pan Am as a Boeing 707 copilot. The plan, hatched as a 19-year-old at the Marine Corps Officer Recruiting Office in lower Manhattan, had, tenuously and with a lot of luck, come together.

Appendix

Hull Loss and/or Fatal Accidents 1965-1968

Between 1965 and 1968 the Navy recorded 286 Marine Corps CH-46s accidents, 26 of which resulted in fatalities or the aircraft were written off due to the extent of damage. This appendix is a summary of those events.

Marble Mountain Air Facility's boneyard

This HMM-164 CH-46A had an engine failure during a night approach with its landing light inoperative and touched down at a high sink rate, buckling the aft fuselage. The accident occurred July 20, 1966, four months after HMM-164 arrived in country.

Crew Related:

Date	Bu No *	Probable Cause
May 9, 1966	151915	CH-34 entered traffic pattern in non-compliance with course rules and descended into CH-46 in landing pattern. Three fatal in CH-34. HOLF Mile Square, CA.
Sept 7, 1966	152546	During night approach to LPH-7 USS Guadalcanal, LPH-7 pilots were warned that they were too low but descent continued into water and helicopter sank. Probable spatial disorientation. All three crew egressed. No serious injuries. N34 deg. 15.7m W77 deg. 21.5m, North Atlantic.
Feb 16, 1968	153348	Helicopter flew into cloud obscured high terrain and struck hillside. Five killed. Vicinity of Pacheco Pass, CA.
Sept 10, 1968	150934	High sink rate with external load caused hard landing. Marble Mountain Air Facility, Vietnam.
Oct 11, 1968	151917	Midair collision. CH-46 climbed into underside of CH-34. Failure to observe orbiting traffic. 12 Fatal*. Hill 52 vicinity of An Hua, Vietnam. * One unaccounted for in wreckage
Nov 3, 1968	153325	Flew into cloud-obscured terrain and struck hillside during medevac mission. Four fatal. Vietnam.

* Bureau Number, essentially the serial number of the aicraft.

Date	Bu No	Probable Cause
Jul 20, 1966	151958	Engine failure during night approach at low altitude. Hard landing. Landing light inoperative due to extension motor failure precluded accurate judgment of height above ground. Stopped descent at 15 feet and dropped hard to the ground. Possible fuel contamination. No injuries. Dong Ha, Vietnam.
Jun 2, 1968	152545	Attempted takeoff while still partially chained to USS Valley Forge LPH-8. Helicopter flipped on side and burned. Ammunition detonated during fire. A/C shoved over the side by deck crane. One fatal, one deck hand serious. South China Sea vicinity.

Maintenance/Material:

Date	Bu No	Probable Cause
Sept 14, 1966	152506	Separation of aft collective pitch yoke assembly due to improper bolt torque. Aft rotors severed fuselage and helicopter dropped into surf and burned. No serious injuries. Marble Mountain Air Facility, Vietnam.
May 1, 1967	150268	Sequential dual engine failure during night approach to hospital ship, USS Sanctuary and subsequent ditching and sinking. 7 fatal. 24 miles north of Chu Lai, Vietnam, South China Sea.

Date	Bu No	Probable Cause
May 3, 1967	152572	Inflight component failure, vicinity Santa Ana, CA. Three* fatal, aircraft destroyed (*incomplete information)
May 12, 1967	152550	Aft transmission failure. Helicopter broke up in flight. Four fatal. South China Sea, 15.5 nm southeast of Marble Mountain Air Facility, Vietnam.
Jun 20, 1967	150936	Power loss after takeoff from USS Princeton LPH5. Ditched at sea and sank. Two fatal (one unknown due to insufficient report information). N15 Deg. 45 Min. E 108 Deg. 31 Min. South China Sea.
Jul 3, 1967	152532	Aft rotor thrust bearing failure due to inappropriate grease lubricant. Insufficient knowledge of lubricant qualities. Lubricant designed for oscillating bearings rather than rotating bearings. Four fatal. Vicinity of Dong Ha, Vietnam.
Jul 28, 1967	151929	Loss of power on one engine followed by loss of power on second engine during relight attempt. Aircraft consumed by post impact fire. Possible inadvertent shutdown of second engine. Copilot sustained concussion. Vietnam.
Aug 31, 1967	152569	Rotor blade failure due to fatigue crack. Inflight breakup. Probable four killed. Vietnam.*

* Incomplete information.

Date	Bu No	Probable Cause
Oct 6, 1967	152517	Forward transmission failure due to lack of lubrication to input pinion bearing caused by clogged oil filter. Structural failure occurred moments after precautionary landing. No injuries. 22 miles southwest of MCAS New River.
Dec 1, 1967	153967	After transmission failure and inflight breakup. Improper sun gear installation. Three killed. Vicinity MCAS New River.
Mar 6, 1968	151943	Dual engine shutdown during post maintenance flight test during fuel dumping and subsequent ditching at sea. Possible inadvertent fuel valves mistakenly switched off, although recovery of wreckage revealed fuel valves on. One fatal. LPH-8, USS Valley Forge, at sea.
Jun 19, 1968	151925	Engine failure.
Jul 2, 1968	153343	Rotor blade failure on base leg of mountain confined area approach followed by inflight separation of aft pylon. A/C struck ground in near vertical nose high attitude and burned. Two fatal, one serious injury. 2000 feet MSL, eight miles north of MCAS El Toro, CA. Maintenance failed to inspect rotor blade at appropriate interval due to administrative error.

Date	Bu No	Probable Cause
Dec 21, 1968	153989	Number 1 engine compressor stall at approx. 200 feet AGL. A/C was below single engine flying speed and settled into trees severing all rotor blades and landed hard with extensive fuselage damage. Compressor erosion and FOD. No injuries. Vicinity An Hoa, Vietnam at 1250 feet MSL.

Unknown/Other Causes:

Date	Bu No	Probable Cause
Oct 6, 1966	151960	Disappeared on flight from Phu Bai to MMAF, Da Nang. Four fatal.
May 28, 1968	151946	Encountered rotor- wash on approach lost rotor RPM and electrical power. Stuck ground, rolled and burned. Four minor injuries. Hoi An, Vietnam.
May 31, 1968	150960	Aircraft struck by "friendly fire" artillery round in flight. One crew injured three fatal. Elephant Valley, west of An Hua, Vietnam.
Jun 19, 1968	153381	* A parachute in the landing zone blew into the rotor system causing the forward rotor head and transmission to separate along with the aft rotor head and vertical shaft and portions of the aft pylon. The aft rotors struck the cockpit. Two fatal (pilot and copilot). Vicinity of Quang Tri, Vietnam. * Incomplete Information.

Source: Department of the Navy,
 Naval History and Heritage Command.

Postscript

Amerca was destined to fight the Vietnam War but in retrospect, it was a huge mistake. Concerns about the threat of Communism after World War II, Soviet expansion into Eastern Europe, the Communist takeover of China in 1949, and the Korean War from 1950 to '53, set the stage for America's involvement. Fears were fanned by exploitive politicians, peaking in the Communist paranoia of the1950s and the McCarthy Hearings in the U.S. Senate, a witch hunt for "Communist agents and sympathizers" alleged to have infiltrated American institutions far and wide. Although Communism with its totalitarian underpinnings proved to be a failed ideological experiment, anxiety about Communist expansionism didn't fade until the Soviet Union finally collapsed in 1991 of its own dysfunctional weight and its failure to match the West's and, particularly, America's economic and military might.

Ho Chi Minh chose to free Vietnam from French colonialism through force under a Communist banner, in part and perhaps largely, because political alternatives were blocked by European powers and not supported by America. The victorious countries of Europe after World War I retained their Asian colonies while the United States, which disdained Europe's colonial exploitation, was nevertheless content with the status quo. Ho Chi Minh's efforts to gain political independence for Vietnam, citing the principles of American democracy, were first rebuffed by President Wilson in 1919 following World War I, and again by President Harry Truman after World War II. By then, Ho Chi Minh was inexorably aligned with and tacitly supported by the Soviet Union and Communist China.

In 1950, the United States, more interested in maintaining the status quo as an alternative to Communist expansion, began providing material support to French forces endeavoring to reassert post-war colonial influence over Vietnam. The French defeat at Dien Bien Phu in 1954 led to the Geneva Accords which divided Vietnam into north and south, the North headed by Ho Chi Minh, and the South by Ngo Dinh Diem, who was aligned with the West. The Geneva Accords stipulated that elections be held in 1956 to determine unification of the country. When the fighting stopped in 1955, one million, mostly Catholic Vietnamese from the north, migrated to the south and about 52,000 Vietnamese moved north. But South Vietnam, fearing an electoral defeat because the bulk of the country's population lived in the north, refused to sign the accords and in 1956, declined to hold the unification vote stipulated in the 1954 Geneva Accords. The North responded by initiating guerrilla warfare in the South to unseat the government and unify the country.

The United States simply viewed South Vietnam as yet another domino in danger of falling to the Communist block and began sending military advisors in 1956. President Kennedy's inaugural address in 1961 set the tone for America's escalating involvement when he said:

"Let every nation know, whether it wishes us well or ill, that we shall pay any price, bear any burden, meet any hardship, support any friend, oppose any foe, in order to assure the survival and success of liberty."

And so American military involvement began in earnest. But Americans underestimated the lives and treasure Ho Chi Minh was willing to sacrifice to unite Vietnam as a Communist society. In the end, even with massive American support, South Vietnam lacked the political and military capacity to deter Ho Chi Minh's military conquest of the south.

According to the Department of Defense, U.S. troop levels increased from 760 in 1959 to over 536,000 in 1968. After that, with increasing resistance to the war at home, U.S. troop involvement gradually decreased until all troops were withdrawn in 1973.

By the end of the conflict in 1975, overall Vietnamese civilian casualties on both sides were estimated by the Vietnamese government in 1995 at two million. Other estimates put the total civilian casualties at 663,000. What is certain is that well over a half million civilian deaths resulted from America's unsuccessful efforts to reverse Ho Chi Minh's vision of uniting Vietnam under a Communist mantle. Atrocities were committed on both sides. Estimates vary widely about Vietnamese war related deaths after 1975 but they range from 400,000 to 2.5 million from all causes.

The Army of the Republic of Vietnam suffered around a quarter million killed with varying estimates well above and below that number. The North Vietnamese and Viet Cong had about 1.1 million killed. American casualties were 58,282 killed in action including prisoners and the missing in action. The wounded numbered 303,644.

The war's ecological damage from defoliants and

ordinance will be the most enduring. Birth defects related to defoliants are another war legacy. To this day, large swaths of Vietnam are severely altered from the effects of defoliants sprayed by U.S. aircraft. Birth defects numbered in the hundreds of thousands. Approximately 25 million acres of cropland were destroyed. Unexploded munitions are continually uncovered and injuries and deaths from these encounters occur routinely. By some estimates, 20,000 people in Vietnam and Laos have been killed or injured by unexploded ordinance since hostilities ceased in 1975.

Thirty-eight years later, Vietnam is still controlled by a repressive Communist government. But a gradual evolution is occurring as a result of market forces, the ease of worldwide communications and geopolitical realities. China, which itself is haltingly morphing to a more open, capitalist society, is increasingly viewed by Vietnam as aggressive and militarily threatening, particularly in the South China Sea. In time, in my view, these realities will move Vietnam to continually improving relations with the U.S. and eventually toward a more free and representative society. A U.S bilateral trade agreement was signed in 2001. A U.S. bilateral air pact was signed in 2003 and direct air service between the two countries began in 2004. A bilateral maritime agreement was signed in 2007. Also in 2007 the U.S. amphibious assault ship Peleliu made a port call in Da Nang with a multinational contingent of medical and engineering personnel. That same year, Vietnamese observers took part in a multinational naval exercise in the South China Sea organized by the U.S. In 2011, U.S. banks agreed to invest 1.5 billion dollars in Vietnamese infrastructure projects. And in 2013 Starbucks announced the opening of its first retail outlet in Hanoi.

As a young U.S. Marine aviator, I fought with and against the Vietnamese who were trapped in time and place in this most difficult and bloody part of their political evolution. I am optimistic that one day, Ho Chi Minh's early idealistic dreams for a Vietnam in the spirit of American democracy will at some point occur. But Vietnam will have paid a horrendously large price to get there and the scars we left on the country will remain for generations.

Bibliography

Bonnie-Sue, A Marine Corps Helicopter Squadron In Vietnam, Marion F. Sturkey, 1996

U.S. Army Medical Department, Office of Medical History, General Medicine and Infectious Diseases, Colonel John J. Deller, 1982

U.S. Marines in Vietnam, An Expanding War, 1966, Jack Shulimson History and Museums Division, Headquarters USMC, Washington, D.C., 1982

The U.S. Marines Fighting the North Vietnamese 1967, Headquarters USMC, Major Gary L. Telfer, USMC, Lt. Col. Lane Rogers, USMC, V. Keith Flemming, Jr., 1984

Accident Reports, Department of the Navy, History and Heritage Command Statistics of Democide, Genocide and Mass Murder Since 1900, R.J. Rummel, School of Law, University of Virginia and Transaction Publishers, Rutgers University, 1997

"Ho Chi Minh: North Vietnam Leader," *Vietnam Magazine* February 1990 Issue, Charles E. Kirkpatrick

Glossary

AK-47   Russian designed assault rifle.

ADF   Automatic direction finder.
               A   compass pointer displaying
               bearing from a radio transmitter.

ARVN   Army of the Republic of Vietnam
               (South Vietnamese Army)

AVCO   Aviation Company

BOQ   Bachelor officers quarters

Click   1000 meters, approximately 3281 ft.
               Military terrain charts are laid out in
               1000 meter grid squares called "clicks."

Collective Lever	Simultaneously changes pitch on all rotor blades.
Cyclic Stick	Controls the direction of rotor blade tip path plane.
D ring	The handle activating parachute deployment.
DI	Drill instructor
DME	Distance measuring equipment. A cockpit TACAN receiver component providing nautical mile distance to a TACAN station.
DMZ	Demilitarized Zone. In Vietnam, the 17th parallel dividing North and South Vietnam.
FCLP	Field carrier landing practice.
FM radio	Radio used to communicate between ground troops and aircraft or between aircraft.
Foxtrot Corpen	The ship's course for flight operations.
GCA	Ground controlled radar approach wherein a ground controller provides glidepath and directional instructions to a landing aircraft.

HAC	Helicopter aircraft commander
Head	Navy/Marine term for a toilet and lavatory facility.
Hill (number)	When not otherwise defined, hills are identified by their height above sea level in meters.
HMM	Marine medium helicopter squadron
HOLF	Helicopter outlying field
IRT	Inter Borough Rapid Transit Company. The company that operated subway lines in New York City before lines were taken over by the city in 1940. For many years after the takeover, the line was still referred to as the IRT.
LPH	Landing platform helicopter. A helicopter aircraft carrier.
LSO	Landing signal officer.
Magneto	An alternating current generator on reciprocating engines providing current to spark plugs.
MARCAD	Marine Corps Aviation cadet
MCAF	Marine Corps air facility

MCAS	Marine Corps Air Station
NATOPS	Naval air training and operating procedures. All navy aircraft have NATOPS manuals defining operating procedures, systems and limitations.
NVA	North Vietnamese Army
OCS	Officers Candidate School
PLC	Platoon Leaders Class (Marine Corps OCS)
PX	Post Exchange
R & R	Rest and recreation. Short term leave provided to personnel in combat zones.
RMI	Radio magnetic indicator. A cockpit instrument providing aircraft heading and radio bearings to ground or air transmitters.
RPM	Revolutions per minute. The aircraft unit of measure for rotating components such as rotor systems or engine compressors and turbines.
SAS	Stabilization augmentation system.

Slipstream	Localized airflow passing over an aircraft.
TACAN	Tactical Air Navigation System. A UHF navigational aid providing bearing and distance in nautical miles from an interrogated ground transmitter.
TAOR	Tactical area of responsibility
UHF	Ultra-high frequency
VC	Viet Cong
VT	Fixed Wing Training Squadron, the V designating a fixed wing squadron.
WESTPAC	Western Pacific

About the Author

Arnold Reiner grew up in the Riverdale section of New York City and entered the Marine Corps Platoon Leader Class Officer program at age 19. Upon receiving his degree in industrial journalism from the University of Bridgeport in 1964, he was commissioned a second lieutenant, entered Navy pilot training, and was designated a Naval Aviator in 1965.

He joined Marine Medium Helicopter Squadron HMM-265, which had recently received the new CH-46A helicopters at the Marine Corps Air Facility New River in Jacksonville, North Carolina, and deployed with the squadron to Vietnam in April, 1966. Later, he served in-country with Marine Medium Helicopter Squadron HMM-164. During his Vietnam tour he was awarded the Purple Heart, 11 Air Medals, the Vietnam Air Gallantry Medal and the Vietnam Service Medal. Returning from Vietnam in June 1967 as a captain, he was an instructor in squadrons HMM-261 and HMM-161 at MCAF New River, training CH-46 pilots for Vietnam duty.

After completing his military obligation, Captain Reiner joined Pan American World Airways as a Boeing 707 copilot flying routes to Europe and South America. Later in his career, he was the director of flight safety at Pan Am and a captain on the Boeing 727 and Airbus A310. In his flight safety role, he wrote numerous articles which were reprinted in airline journals and safety publications around the world. As a member of the International Air Transport Association Safety Advisory Committee, and U.S. Air Transport Association Safety Committee he was instrumental in fostering safety practices which are today commonplace among the world's major airlines. When Pan Am sold its European routes to Delta Air Lines in 1991, Reiner joined Delta and retired as a Boeing 727 captain in 2000. Today, Captain Reiner lives in Pensacola, Florida with his wife, Cascille, of 46 years.

Captain Reiner

CPSIA information can be obtained at www.ICGtesting.com
Printed in the USA
BVOW02s0341150615

404082BV00002B/15/P

9 781604 520842